Lady In Waiting
Meditations For the Heart

DEVELOPING YOUR LOVE RELATIONSHIPS

Lady In Waiting
Meditations For the Heart

DEVELOPING YOUR LOVE RELATIONSHIPS

DEBBY JONES AND JACKIE KENDALL

Treasure House

An Imprint of

Destiny Image® Publishers, Inc.
P.O. Box 310
Shippensburg, PA 17257-0310

"For where your treasure is, there will your heart be also."
Matthew 6:21

ISBN 0-7684-3034-8

For Worldwide Distribution
Printed in the U.S.A.

This book and all other Destiny Image, Revival Press, MercyPlace, Fresh Bread, Destiny Image Fiction, and Treasure House books are available at Christian bookstores and distributors worldwide.

For a U.S. bookstore nearest you, call **1-800-722-6774**.
For more information on foreign distributors, call **717-532-3040**.
Or reach us on the Internet:
www.destinyimage.com

A Word From the Authors

Have you ever noticed the funny way a pigeon walks? His head moves forward, he stops, then he takes a step. I have read that a pigeon's eyes do not focus unless his head is still...therefore, he focuses—then steps. We could learn a lot from this "pigeon walk."

Sometimes our lives seem to get out of control and our hearts are injured and our steps unsure. We lose focus and life comes apart at the seams. This Journal is designed to help us keep focus—step by step and day by day.

Proverbs 3:5-6 are key words to live by with regard to our steps. "Trust in the Lord with all your heart...." How much misdirection and pain could we avoid if we trusted in and were daily assured of our God's awesome love for us? "And do not lean on your own understanding...." What trouble could we avoid if we went to the all-knowing God for daily direction and wisdom instead of fretting, planning and, worrying? "In all your ways acknowledge Him..." This is our focus for each step. And the promise? "He will make your paths straight."

It really doesn't matter how much we "know"—it matters how much we "live." This type of journaling through the years has helped me to live more of what I know. I pray that, as you use this spiritual journey tool, you will catch yourself refocusing before each step.

May God richly bless your "walk" with Him!
— Debby Jones

Thirty years ago, my spiritual mentor shared the secret of her incredible life with Jesus, and I have tried to *live* the secret since she shared it on that memorable summer day in 1972:

"There is no success, no happiness, and no fulfillment in life apart from a consistent, daily growing relationship with Jesus through the Word."

I have watched thousands of women try to find happiness, success, and fulfillment without spending quiet time with Jesus...and I can testify that their efforts have been in vain.

— Jackie Kendall

Helpful Tips for the Lady In Waiting

The purpose of this journal is to introduce you to a fresh and exciting way of enhancing your personal life and enriching your spiritual journey. We have taken some of the most energizing quotes from *Lady in Waiting*, mixed in great motivational thoughts from classic writers of the past, and have come up with a delectable spiritual meal that will satisfy the appetite of the hungry soul.

It is not enough to simply read the individual quotes, write a few words, and then move on to the next page. The authors and the publisher encourage you to prayerfully meditate on these powerful truths. As you do so, this journal can then become a resource that will help promote you to new heights of intimacy with the Lord Jesus and prepare you for deeper levels of relationships.

To Learn His Presence

It is our desire that this journal will help you live in the presence of the Lord every day. It is not intended to simply add new truth to a bag of theological truth that is already full; rather, it is our expectation that it will bring you to a place of new experiences with your God.

It will require that you spend time carefully considering the significance and implications of each individual quote. Let its spiritual vibrations resonate in your heart. Contemplate their spiritual meaning as you apply them to your life, ultimately letting them lead you to a quiet place of prayer and communion with your Divine Lover, the Lord Jesus.

Begin Your Journey

Few of us have the opportunity for quiet meditation and personal contemplation every day. Therefore, the pages are not dated. It is important that you use this journal when you have the time to give yourself to prayer and meditation. It will not help you if you simply make this experience a part of a daily regimen of religious duty.

To begin the journey, it is imperative that you find a quiet place where you can get alone with your journal, your Bible, and your Lord. Read each quote several times, making sure that you have captured the essence of the writer's thoughts. Do not be content with a casual glance before quickly moving on to the next quote. Allow the Spirit of the Lord to enter your thought processes and bring fresh insight. Let the words become a prayer that is formed on your lips.

The practice of contemplative prayer is certainly a lost art in our Western society. We are used to having our spiritual food gathered, prepared, cooked, and delivered to our table by our favorite preachers of the day. This journal will help you break out of this spiritual rut.

You might want to talk to your friends about a quote and get their thoughts and reactions. How about memorizing a portion of the quote so that you can reflect on it during the day?

Come back to these words several times. Do not be satisfied with only one look. Often, days down the road, fresh meaning and application will come to you.

Here are a few reflective questions that will help guide you in your meditations:

What is the main focus and intent of the author's words?

How does this concept apply to my life?

What Scripture verses will lead me into further application of the truth?

What circumstances have I gone through that enrich the meaning of the statements?

Are there any particular areas of my life that need adjustment so that I can move into a new dimension of experiencing the power of this truth?

What is preventing me right now from entering into the reality of this compelling insight?

How can I form the truth of this quote into a personal prayer to the Lord?

Before you begin, start with this quote from Madame Guyon's book, *A Short and Very Easy Method of Prayer*:

Meditative reading is the choosing some important practical or speculative truth, always preferring the practical, and proceeding thus: whatever truth you have chosen, read only a small portion of it; endeavoring to taste and digest it, to extract the essence and substance of it; and proceed no farther while any savor or relish remains in the passage: then take up your book again, and proceed as before, seldom reading more than half a page at a time.

It is not the quantity that is read, but the manner of reading that yields us profit. Those who read fast, reap no more advantage, than a bee would by only skimming over the surface of the flower, instead of waiting to penetrate into it, and extract its sweets. Much reading is rather for scholastic subjects, than divine truths; to receive profit from spiritual books, we must read as I have described; and I am certain that if that method were pursued, we should become gradually habituated to prayer by our reading, and more fully disposed for its exercise.

(Madame Jeanee Guyon, *A Short and Very Easy Method of Prayer*, Ch. II. 3 Jan. 2002 <http://www.passtheword.org/DIALOGS-FROM-THE-PAST/methodofprayer.htm>)

Special Note

Unless otherwise noted, passages are taken directly from Debby Jones and Jackie Kendall's book *Lady in Waiting* (Shippensburg, Pennsylvania: Destiny Image Publishers, 1995).

Contents

Day: _Tues day_ Date: _1/6/09_ Time: _11:30 pm_ Location: _my room at home_

Fulfillment

Fulfillment

Have you assumed that your ultimate fulfillment would be found in marriage? Have you privately entertained the notion that the only satisfied women are married women? Have you been expecting your career to satisfy you until you are married? If you have answered "yes" to any of these questions, then you have a prospect of disillusionment looming in the future. "...A woman becomes a woman when she becomes what God wants her to be."* This priceless truth can help keep your perspective clear in relation to true fulfillment in life. Too many Christian women think that the inner longings of their heart relate only to love, marriage, and motherhood. Look a little closer and see if that longing isn't ultimately for Jesus. Gary Chapman once remarked, "I feel very strongly that marriage is not a higher calling than the single state. Happy indeed are those people, married or single, who have discovered that happiness is not found in marriage but in a right relationship with God." Fulfillment for a Christian woman begins with the Lordship of Christ in every area of her life.

*Kenneth G. Smith, *Learning to Be a Woman* (Downers Grove, Illinois: InterVarsity Press, 1972), backcover, as cited in *Lady in Waiting*.)

God, there are so many places in my life that you are not Lord of. Show them to me when I am ready to work on giving each one to You. Marriage scares me right now. I would not want to be tied down

Now Lord I want to be free to move and live where I choose. I want to live with my sister later on in life in an apartment that looks over the ocean in San Diego. Although, You probably have much bigger, exciting, and wonderful plans for me compared to my humble ones. You can have that dream. Do what you want with it. Here's another: getting paid well in a flexible job that I enjoy (in math). I'll be poor if that's what's best for me. The thing is I want the benefits of marriage right now. How do I wait so long? Help keep my mind off of it and to give it to you.

Fulfillment for a Christian woman begins with the Lordship of Christ in every area of her life.

Day: _____ Date: _____ Time: _____ Location: _____

Journey Away From Rituals

Ruth moved from a false religion into the only true and eternal relationship. Too many women have been involved in a form of religious worship, but have never had a vital, growing relationship with Jesus…Has your faith been a lifeless ritual rather than a vital love relationship with Jesus? Why not spend some of your free hours as a single woman beginning a journey away from rituals into a deep relationship with Jesus Christ?

One single woman expressed this vital relationship with Jesus in the following way: "I desired that my relationship with the Lord be an adventure. One where I would find out what pleased Him and then do it, devoting as much energy to Jesus as I would in a relationship with a boyfriend. I am falling more in love with Jesus every day." Do you know more about pleasing a boyfriend than you do about pleasing the Lord Jesus?

_____

_____

_____

_____

_____

_____

_____

_____

_____

_____

_____

_____

_____

_____

_____

_____

_____

_____

_____

_____

_____

_____

_____

_____

_____

*Has your faith been a lifeless ritual rather than
a vital love relationship with Jesus?*

Day: _____ Date: _____ Time: _____ Location: _____

His Blueprints

Another costly aspect of Ruth's choice was the time frame in Israel's history. It was the age of the judges, a period of time described as "do your own thing"; "Everyone did what was right in his own eyes" (Judg. 21:25b). Ruth chose not only to break her family cycle, but also to challenge the lifestyle that many in Israel embraced. She wanted God's will, not hers; His blueprints, not her elementary scribbling; God's assignment, not her foolish plans

Whenever a single woman decides to abandon herself completely to Jesus, as Ruth did, she will find herself out of step with society and, sometimes, even with her friends. A single woman today needs the boldness to challenge and break the cycle of the "American way" that exalts a relationship with a man as an answer to life. This "American way" blurs the reality of the ultimate answer to life found in a deep relationship with Jesus Christ. A modern-day Ruth wrote: " My deep satisfaction from my commitment to Jesus is constantly challenged by other believers. They treat me like some kind of Neanderthal, definitely out of step with the 90's woman."

_____

_____

_____

_____

_____

_____

_____

_____

_____

_____

_____

_____

_____

_____

_____

_____

_____

_____

_____

_____

_____

_____

_____

_____

_____

_____

*…His blueprints, not her elementary scribbling; God's
assignment, not her foolish plans…*

Day: _____ Date: _____ Time: _____ Location: _____

Tightly Bound

Ruth came to the God of Israel after years of living in darkness, but He gladly received her service even though she was a Moabite foreigner. She bound herself to the service of the Lord, interweaving her service with Him like the braiding of a heavy rope. Isaiah 56:6-7 (NIV) refers to a foreigner binding himself (or herself) to the Lord and His willingly receiving their "diligent" service: "And foreigners who bind themselves to the Lord to serve Him...these I will bring to My holy mountain...".

Are you tightly bound to the Lord, serving Him diligently, or has your relationship and service been unraveling over the years as you continue to be single and not married? Has resentment and self-pity unraveled what used to be a tightly woven labor for the Lord? You must be sensitive to the things and situations that distract you from redeeming your free time. "Whatever might blur the vision God had given [Elisabeth Elliot] of His work, whatever could distract or deceive or tempt others to seek anything but the Lord Jesus Himself she tried to eliminate."*

*Elisabeth Elliot, *A Chance to Die* (Old Tappan, New Jersey: Fleming H. Revell Company, 1987), p. 117, as cited in *Lady In Waiting*.

_____

_____

_____

_____

_____

_____

_____

_____

_____

_____

_____

_____

_____

_____

_____

_____

_____

_____

_____

_____

_____

_____

_____

_____

_____

Are you tightly bound to the Lord,
serving Him diligently...?"

Day: _____ Date: _____ Time: _____ Location: _____

Mother Teresa

She was born Agnes Gonxha Bojaxhiu in 1910 in Skopje, Yugoslavia (now Macedonia). In 1928 she decided to become a nun and went to Dublin, Ireland, to join the Sisters of Loreto. From there she went to the Loreto convent in Darjeeling, India.

In 1929 she began to teach geography at St. Mary's High School for Girls in Calcutta. In those days the streets of Calcutta were crowded with beggars, lepers, and the homeless. Unwanted infants were regularly abandoned on the streets or in garbage bins. In 1946, Mother Teresa felt the need to abandon her teaching position to care for the needy in the slums of Calcutta.

Initially focusing her efforts on poor children in the streets, Mother Teresa taught them how to read and how to care for themselves. Many former students of St. Mary's eventually joined her order. Each girl who joined was required to devote her life to serving the poor without accepting any material reward in return.

(Mother Theresa. January 22, 1997. October 8, 1999. <http://www.nalejandria.com/utopia/english/
MotherTheresa-eng.htm/> as cited in Don Milam, *The Lost Passions of Jesus*
[Shippensburg, Pennsylvania: MercyPlace, 1999], p. 131)

My True Community

Keep giving Jesus to your people not by words, but by your example, by your being in love with Jesus, by radiating his holiness and spreading his fragrance of love everywhere you go. Just keep the joy of Jesus as your strength. Be happy and

at peace. Accept whatever he gives and give what
ever he takes with a big smile. You belong to him.

...

My true community is the poor— their security
is my security, their health is my health. My home
is among the poor, and not only the poor, but
the poorest of them: the people no one will go
near because they are filthy and suffering from
contagious diseases, full of germs and vermin—
infested; the people who can't go to church
because they can't go out naked; the people who
can no longer eat because they haven't the
strength; the people who lie down in the street,
knowing they are going to die, while others look
away and pass them by; the people who no longer
cry because their tears have run dry!

The Lord wants me exactly where I am— he
will provide the answers.

(Eileen Egan and Kathleen Egan, *Suffering Into Joy* [Ann Arbor, Michigan: Servan Publications, 1994], pp. 22, 89)

_____

_____

_____

_____

_____

_____

Accept whatever He gives—and give whatever He takes
with a big smile. You belong to Him.

Day: _____ Date: _____ Time: _____ Location: _____

Life on Hold

Some singles see the lack of a mate as God denying them something for a more "noble purpose"—*a cross to bear*! Our selfish nature tends to focus on what we do not have rather than on what we do have—free time—that can be used for others and ourselves. Is your life on hold until you have someone to hold?

…Have you experienced…a crushing emotional blow?… Psalm 34:18 says, "The Lord is near to the brokenhearted, and saves those who are crushed in spirit." [A] brokenhearted woman had put her life on hold after her husband divorced her. Such a response is understandable, but…this now single woman decided to take her broken heart, her empty arms, and her loneliness and give them to Jesus. In exchange, Jesus taught her how to resist feeling sorry for herself and how to stop living in the arena of bitterness. After she made the choice of recklessly abandoning herself to Jesus as Lord, she was free to serve Him. This once brokenhearted single woman has been transformed into a fearless servant of the Lord….

Have you also put your life on hold? Do you have an excuse for not serving Jesus?

_____

_____

_____

_____

_____

_____

_____

_____

_____

_____

_____

_____

_____

_____

_____

_____

_____

_____

_____

_____

_____

Is your life on hold until you have someone to hold?

Day: _____ Date: _____ Time: _____ Location: _____

Adjust Your Vision

It is doubtful that there could ever be a better time to serve Jesus than this "moment" of singleness. Rather than wasting precious moments fantasizing about an earthly lover, take advantage of your free hours each day to serve the Lord of Heaven. If you are frustrated and distracted, rather than fruitfully serving Jesus, then ask Him right now to adjust your vision.

...Don't worry about that certain guy you have had your eye on for a while. If he is God's best for you, he will be there when you return....

Is there an opportunity of service that you have avoided because you can't give up your "post on the castle wall" looking for your knight in shining armor?...As you get older, you assume more obligations and responsibilities that demand your time and attention. Such distractions will make serving Jesus even more difficult. Have you given Jesus full reign over your time?

Limitless ministry opportunities exist for the Lady of Diligence. These ministries are available right this moment. They do not demand a Bible college education. The only requirement is a single woman who desires to use her time wisely in ministry.

_____

_____

_____

_____

_____

_____

_____

_____

_____

_____

_____

_____

_____

_____

_____

_____

_____

_____

_____

_____

_____

Is there an opportunity of service that you have avoided because you can't give up your "post on the castle wall" looking for your knight in shining armor?...

Day: _____ Date: _____ Time: _____ Location: _____

His Script

God providentially directed Ruth to the field of Boaz. You find this divine encounter in the second chapter of Ruth, verse 3: "...and she happened to come to the portion of the field belonging to Boaz...." The verb *happened* in Hebrew means "chanced upon." This leaves no room for manipulation. She had a chance and her chance transported her into the center of God's will and right to Boaz's field....

If Jesus wants you married, He will orchestrate the encounter. You have nothing to fear except getting in His way and trying to "write the script" rather than following His. Jesus does have your best interest at heart. He desires to bless you by giving you the best. Sometimes what you perceive as the best is nothing more than a generic version. Consider His wisdom and love in comparison to your own wisdom and self-love. In whom are you going to trust—all Wisdom and Everlasting Love or little ol' finite you? Ever since the Garden of Eden, women have often felt they could and should know as much as God. Much pain in our world has resulted from dependence on our wisdom rather than on our Father's.

_____

_____

_____

_____

_____

_____

_____

_____

_____

_____

_____

_____

_____

_____

_____

_____

_____

_____

_____

_____

_____

You have nothing to fear except getting in His way and trying
to "write the script" rather than following His.

Day: _____ Date: _____ Time: _____ Location: _____

Susanna Wesley

Susanna (Annesley) Wesley was born on January 20, 1669, in London, England and is most known for being the mother of the famous Wesley boys, John and Charles. Susanna was the youngest of 25 children. Her father was a minister and often let Susanna take part in theological discussions with his minister friends.

At the age of 19, Susanna married 26-year-old Samuel Wesley. He was a newly ordained Anglican priest who was named rector of the Epworth parish. During the absence of her husband Samuel, Susanna began a Bible study within her home. Neighbors, family, and friends soon heard of the Bible studies and the crowd soon grew to over 200 hungry souls.

Susanna regularly spent an hour in prayer and Bible reading every day. This practice was built into the lives of her children and bore fruit in their powerful preaching and passionate prayers.

Susanna passed away on July 25, 1742.

A Life Worthy of Eternity

This life is nothing in comparison of eternity; so very inconsiderable, and withal so wretched, that it is not worthwhile to be, if we were to die as the beasts. What mortal would sustain the pains, the wants, the disappointments, the cares, and thousands of calamities we must often suffer here? But when we consider this as a probationary state... and that if we wisely behave ourselves here, if we purify our souls from all corrupt and inordinate affections, if we can, by the divine assistance, recover the image of God (moral goodness), which we lost in Adam, and attain to a heavenly temper and disposition of mind, full of the love of God, etc., then we justly think that this life is an effect of the inconceivable goodness of God towards us...

I have such a vast inexpressible desire of your salvation, and such dreadful apprehensions of your failing in a work of so great importance; and do moreover know by experience how hard a thing it is to be a Christian, that I cannot for fear, I cannot but most earnestly press you and conjure you, over and over again, to give the most earnest heed to what you have already learned, lest at any time you let slip the remembrance of your final happiness, or forget what you have to do in order to attain it.

(George J. Stevenson, *Memorials of the Wesley Family*, Partridge, 1876, p. 185, as cited in Arnold Dallimore, *Susanna Wesley* [Grand Rapids, Michigan: Baker Books, 1993], pp. 91-92)

...if we can, by the divine assistance, recover the image of God... then we justly think that this life is an effect of the inconceivable goodness of God towards us...

Day: _____ Date: _____ Time: _____ Location: _____

Become a Princess

When you picture the perfect man for you, what is your prince like? Do you see a man devoted to God? A man of character—teachable, loyal, faithful, gentle, and kind? What kind of woman do you think this godly man desires to marry—a shallow woman or a woman full of charm who knows how to dress and capture other men's attention? Is this the one he imagines he will one day want to spend the rest of his life with—the mother of his heirs? No way!!

To marry a prince, you must first become a princess. To marry into royalty, you must be appropriately prepared. Even Diana, the Princess of Wales, had to go through a period of "waiting and preparing" before marrying Prince Charles. She had to learn how to properly act, dress, and speak so she would honor the royal family. Is it any wonder that a heavenly princess must prepare inwardly for the calling to which she will give her life? As you set your attention on developing godly character, Christ will change you into the beautiful princess He created you to be.

_____

_____

_____

_____

_____

_____

_____

_____

_____

_____

_____

_____

_____

_____

_____

_____

_____

_____

_____

_____

_____

_____

_____

_____

_____

To marry a prince, you must first become a princess.

Day: _____ Date: _____ Time: _____ Location: _____

Your Destiny

Do you think your ideals and standards are too high? Do you feel the pressure to compromise and settle for the generic version of life? Ruth lived in an era that was exactly like modern America. Judges 21:25 describes the era in which she lived: "In those days there was no king in Israel; everyone did what was right in his own eyes." We too live in a culture where it seems that no one fears God and people just "do their own thing."

You, like Ruth, will be greatly affected by your choices. Ruth's wise choices allowed her to break a godless family cycle and begin a new cycle that the Word of God triumphantly records. God has not changed—and neither have men. The high standards in God's Word are not irrelevant, but completely applicable to finding God's best for your life. Choices, guided by your convictions rather than by chance, determine your destiny....

You cannot make good choices without proper, biblical convictions. Don't carelessly leave your dating/relating standards to chance. Too much depends on your decisions in this area.

_____

_____

_____

_____

_____

_____

_____

_____

_____

_____

_____

_____

_____

_____

_____

_____

_____

_____

*Choices, guided by your convictions rather than by chance,
determine your destiny…*

Day: _____ Date: _____ Time: _____ Location: _____

Back to the Basics

May we go back to the basics for just a moment? What is a conviction and how does one develop biblical convictions? A conviction is a standard that serves as a springboard for your choices. Consider where your standards, in the area of relating and dating, originated. Are your standards based more on Hollywood's terms of love and romance, or have you allowed God's Holy Word to shape your perspective?

The Lady of Conviction gives the Lord permission to renew her mind on a daily basis. She spends time searching the Word of God for standards that will guide her safely to God's best…She has surrendered her mind to a new persuasion: God's perspective on love and romance. The convictions that she establishes, based on the Word, allow her to resist being squeezed into the mold of this world. She is a non-conformist in a biblical sense, as in Romans 12:2 (NIV) which says, "Do not conform any longer to the pattern of this world, but be transformed by the renewing of your mind. Then you will be able to test and approve what God's will is—His good, pleasing and perfect will."

_____

_____

_____

_____

_____

_____

_____

_____
_____
_____
_____
_____
_____
_____
_____
_____
_____
_____
_____
_____
_____
_____
_____
_____
_____
_____

The Lady of Conviction gives the Lord permission to renew her mind on a daily basis.

Day: _____ Date: _____ Time: _____ Location: _____

A Need, A Right, A Completion

Every single woman must at some point come to grips with the fact that not all women will marry. Marriage is not a need, though God chooses to let marriage meet some needs a woman may have. Marriage is not a right, though God chooses to plan marriage for the majority of women. Marriage does not complete a person, though women who properly marry find that marriage rounds out some of their weaknesses. If marriage were a need, right, or completion for women, then all godly women would marry. There are many examples of true, God-honoring women who had no earthly mate but were still Ladies of Patience.

…

Don't let your impatient longings rob you of the life God wants to bless you with as a single. Realize you do not need marriage for happiness or a full life. If you are holding onto marriage as a right, relinquish this right so it will not keep you from God's fullest blessings. God knows what is best for you. His timing is perfect and He will take care of His Lady of Patience.

_____

_____

_____

_____

_____

_____

_____

_____

_____

_____

_____

_____

_____

_____

_____

_____

_____

_____

_____

_____

_____

_____

_____

_____

_____

_____

*If marriage were a need, right, or completion for women, then
all godly women would marry.*

Day: _____ Date: _____ Time: _____ Location: _____

Basilea Schlink

Basilea (Dr. Klara) Schlink was born in 1904. Her education included social welfare training and a doctorate in psychology. She was a leader of the Women's German Student Christian Movement and bravely stood against Nazi policy during the Hitler regime. She risked her life during World War II, publicly speaking out on the unique destiny of Israel as God's people. Mother Basilea appeared two different times before the German Gestapo for boldly proclaiming Jesus Christ as Lord; she was released despite her unwavering stance. As Mother Basilea and another leader, Mother Martyria, led Bible studies (even teaching the Old Testament that was forbidden by the Nazis) for young people, they began to see revival. The young girls encountered God in a fresh way; His holiness, His justice, His Lordship were experienced anew. Those who were lukewarm in their Christianity repented; hidden sins were confessed and forgiveness flowed.

(Adapted from "Who is M. Basilea Schlink? Who is M. Martyria Madauss?" 04 April 2001.
21 Jan. 2002 <http://www.Kanaan.org/Mother.htm>)

First Love, Divided Love

Jesus, who so often says 'Whoever loves Me . . .' and asks 'Do you love Me?' is concerned about our LOVE! He is concerned about a special kind of love. It is the love which is shadowed in the relationship between a bride and her bridegroom; that is, it is an exclusive love, a love which places the beloved, the bridegroom, above all other loves, in the first place. As a Bridegroom, Jesus has a claim to 'First love'. He who has loved us so much wants to possess us completely with everything we are and have. Jesus gave Himself wholly and completely for us. Now His love is yearning for us to surrender ourselves and everything that we are to Him, so that He can really be our "First love." So long as our love for Him is a divided love, so long as our heart is bound to family, possessions, or the like, He will not count our love to be genuine. Divided love is of so little value to Him that He will not enter into a bond of love with such a soul, for this bond presupposes a full mutual love. Because our love is so precious to Jesus, because He yearns for our love, He waits for our uncompromising commitment.

(Basilea Schlink, "Bridal Love" ©2001 The Watchword. 3 Jan. 2002
<http://www.watchword.org/schlink/ww29d.html>)

_____

_____

_____

_____

_____

_____

_____

_____

_____

_____

_____

As a Bridegroom, Jesus has a claim to "first love".

Day: _____ Date: _____ Time: _____ Location: _____

True Love

Seeking God is very similar to developing a friendship. You talk a lot, you listen, you write each other letters, you think about each other, you find out what the other likes and does not like, and you try to do things that please that person. The more you spend time together, the more intimately you know your friend. And the more intimately you know your friend, the greater your love will be. It works the same way with your relationship with God.

Jeremiah 29:12-13 promises that a woman who diligently seeks God with all her heart will find Him. Your heart is the key to devotion to God. A halfhearted search is not sufficient. This means you cannot seek God while you do your own thing.

Is God demanding too much to require that you seek Him with all your heart? No way!...

...giving Christ your heart means you are not free to give it away to other things or people that come into your life (in idolatry).... Devotion to the Lord Jesus Christ is giving everything or nothing at all. Your devotion to Christ must be a serious commitment....

_____

_____

_____

_____

_____

_____

_____

_____

_____

_____

_____

_____

_____

_____

_____

_____

_____

_____

_____

_____

_____

_____

_____

_____

Devotion to the Lord Jesus Christ is
giving everything or nothing at all.

Day: _____ Date: _____ Time: _____ Location: _____

Choose: Him or What He Can Give

Many seek God, but only for His hand. They don't want God as much as they want something from God, such as a man, happiness, or a family. This impure search for God is limited to what you can get. It is more of a self-love than a God-love. This seeking will end in misery, not in the union of love you desire. God…knows your motives. To grow in your knowledge of God, you must seek God correctly, which means you must also seek God with a pure heart.

A woman with a pure heart for God does not focus on what He gives, but delights in who He is. She seeks God's *face*, not just His *hand*. Would you want someone to say he loves you just so you would do something for him? To find God, you must seek Him with pure motives. Seek Him for who He is, not just for what He can do for you.…

…

Singleness does not have to be a curse.…Singleness puts you in an advantageous position because, more than likely, you have much more time to seek the Lord now than you will ever have if you marry.

_____

_____

_____

_____

_____

_____

_____

_____

_____

_____

_____

_____

_____

_____

_____

_____

_____

_____

_____

_____

_____

_____

_____

_____

_____

_____

_____

. . . you must seek God correctly, which means you must also
seek God with a pure heart.

Day: _____ Date: _____ Time: _____ Location: _____

Your Gift

Since sex is desirable, why not have sex?…

God wants you to be a Lady of Purity because He wants to protect you from the consequences that sex before marriage brings. These consequences can be physical, emotional, relational, and spiritual.…

Have you secretly opened a Christmas gift before Christmas Day and rewrapped it, putting it back under the tree? How thrilling and exciting it was when you saw the surprise. But what about the "big day" when the gifts were supposed to be opened for the first time? Where was the excitement when you opened your gift? The gift did not seem quite as special because it had already been opened for the first time. Each woman receives one "first time." God desires for your precious gift to be given to a committed lover who will cherish, keep, and protect you in marriage. God wants you and your gift to this man to be treasured and cherished, not trampled and conquered. Song of Solomon 8:4 (NIV) says, … "Do not arouse or awaken love until it so desires." God wants to protect you from losing your virginity.

_____

_____

_____

_____

_____

_____

_____

_____

_____

_____

_____

_____

_____

_____

_____

_____

_____

_____

_____

_____

_____

_____

God desires for your precious gift to be given to a committed lover who will cherish, keep, and protect you in marriage.

Day: _____ Date: _____ Time: _____ Location: _____

Hannah More

Born in 1745 in Bristol, England, Hannah More was to become a champion of the disenfranchised of the world. Instead of quiet domesticity, in obscurity, Hannah blazed a trail for women. As a powerful writer she earned a fortune which she used to set up a cottage industry that printed millions of moral tracts that were distributed around the world. She became friends with John Newton, the ex-slave trader, who became her mentor. She joined in with William Wilberforce in the battle against the slave trade.

She has the honor of making English ladies the foremost agent in the education of the poor. The intensity of her love for the Lord Jesus was reflected in a life given for His people.

What an example of balance: the hearts of Mary and Martha beating within the same bosom. Hannah More proves that you can be passionate about His presence and at the same time be a servant to fellow man.

(Tommy Tenney, *God's Favorite House Journal* [Shippensburg, Pennsylvania: Fresh Bread, 2000], p. 25)

Do We Really Love God?

Our love to God arises out of our emptiness;
God's love to us out of His fulness. Our
impoverishment draws us to that power which can
relieve and to that goodness which can bless us.
His overflowing love delights to make us partakers
of the bounties He graciously imparts. We can
only be said to love God when we endeavour to
glorify Him, when we desire a participation of His

nature, when we study to imitate His perfections.

We are sometimes inclined to suspect the love of God to us, while we too little suspect our own lack of love to Him.... When the heart is devoted to God, we do not need to be perpetually reminded of our obligations to obey Him. They present themselves spontaneously and we fulfill them readily. We think not so much of the service as of the One served. [The motivation which suggests the work inspires the pleasure.] The performance is the gratification, and the omission is both a pain to the conscience and wound to the affections....

Though we cannot be always thinking of God, we may be always employed in His service. There must be intervals of our communion with Him, but there must be not intermission of our attachment to Him.

(Hannah More, *The Religion of the Heart* [Burlington, New Jersey: D. Allison & Co., 1811], updated by Donald L. Milam Jr., pp. 27, 33, 85-86, as cited in Tommy Tenney, *Mary's Prayers and Martha's Recipes* [Shippensburg, Pennsylvania: Fresh Bread, 2002], pp. 19-20)

_____

_____

_____

_____

Our love to God arises out of our emptiness;
God's love to us out of His fulness.

Day: _____ Date: _____ Time: _____ Location: _____

Don't Give Too Easily

Don't let your heart be given away too easily. If a man says he loves you, you don't have to echo the phrase. To men these three words can mean all kinds of things, like "I lust for you" or "I want you to kiss me." Or maybe he just can't think of anything else to say at the moment!... Gradually those "I love you's" can trap you emotionally and lead you on physically. To guard the key to your heart, make a commitment to say you love someone only if you love him with a committed love, not a casual love feeling. You will remain much more in control of your friendship. Real love will have time to blossom and grow without those three words. Guard and save them to be whispered when God reveals it is time. What a gift to tell your fiancé, "You are the first person I have ever said this to: 'I love you.' " Give meaning to those precious words, and you may use them and hear them with fondness through many happy years of marriage.

There's a second step you can take to guard your purity. It's a radical statement, but save all your kisses for your future husband....

A woman's kiss or embrace is not just another way of saying thank you! A kiss should say something more intimate.

_____

_____

_____

_____

_____

_____

_____

_____

_____

_____

_____

_____

_____

_____

_____

_____

_____

_____

_____

_____

_____

_____

_____

_____

. . . save all your kisses for your future husband.

Day: _____ Date: _____ Time: _____ Location: _____

Dating Standards

Don't set standards "as you go." Emotions can be tricky. You must make wise choices before the "flutters" and "heartthrobs" become so loud you cannot hear yourself think. Write them down and read them often! Commit them to God regularly in prayer.

...Here are some examples of "dating standards" that many godly women have made. They will help you resist the pressure too "open the gift" too early....

I will date only growing Christian men. (You will most likely marry a man you date. This is important!!)

I will concentrate on the friendship—not romance. (Don't be tricked!)

I will not spend time with him at home when we are alone.

I will not give kisses and hugs freely.

I will not lie down beside a man.

...

Women are easily turned on by words....Another way to protect your purity is to stand on guard when you hear "sweet talk."...

...words have trapped many ladies—beware! When you catch yourself rationalizing what you are doing and assuring yourself you are in control, make a second check. You'll be glad you did.

_____

_____

_____

_____

_____

_____

_____

_____

_____

_____

_____

_____

_____

_____

_____

_____

_____

_____

_____

_____

_____

Don't set standards "as you go."

Day: _____ Date: _____ Time: _____ Location: _____

It's Not Too Late

...If you are reading this "after the fact" and are dealing with the guilt of the lost gift, do not be discouraged. Although it is true that there is only one first time, God is the God of the first-time experience. Let Him heal your broken heart through forgiveness. Agree with God that you have sinned and leave the sin before Him. Then guard yourself from entering into that sin pattern again. Learn a valuable lesson, but do not continue to beat yourself with condemnation. Jesus paid for those sins at Calvary. Do not continue to allow yourself or the enemy to defeat you with remembering a sin once you have confessed it to God and those you have offended. There may be consequences of your sin, but you do not have to live with the guilt of it.

...

Even though you have been freed from the guilt by confession, do not use it as an opportunity to continue in sin or to leave yourself open to temptation. Continue to choose freedom over sin's mastery. Lay aside every encumbrance and the sin that so easily entangles you and run with endurance the race set before you (see Heb. 12:1).

_____

_____

_____

_____

_____

_____

_____

_____

_____

_____

_____

_____

_____

_____

_____

_____

_____

_____

_____

_____

_____

_____

*Lay aside every encumbrance and the sin that so easily
entangles you and run with endurance the race set before you.*

Day: _____ Date: _____ Time: _____ Location: _____

Deficit of a Father's Love

Women tend to struggle with insecurity because of the unique way God created them. God made every little girl with the need to love and be loved by her earthly father. God designed His world with a picture of a family as the theme. The father protects, loves, and cares for his wife and their children. The ideal earthly father models the gentle, nurturing love of the heavenly Father. Many young women in our society did not have a father who followed God's design. This God-given need for a father's love caused a deficit in their lives.

...

As a little girl, you may remember feeling the desire to be cherished, loved, and accepted by your daddy. If he failed to show that love to you in God's way, perhaps you continued to search for a man who would. No man, not even a husband, can fill the need you have for secure love. Only Jesus, who "is the same yesterday and today yes and forever," will never disappoint or fail you (Heb. 13:8).

...the man you marry cannot meet your need for security. Only God's love brings security.

_____

_____

_____

_____

_____

_____

_____

_____

_____

_____

_____

_____

_____

_____

_____

_____

_____

_____

_____

_____

_____

_____

_____

_____

_____

. . . the man you marry cannot meet your need for security.
Only God's love brings security.

Day: _____ Date: _____ Time: _____ Location: _____

Basilea Schlink

Waiting for Our Love

Jesus is yearning to have fellowship with us and to hear words of love drop from our lips. He is waiting for us. He wants us to be close to Him. He wants to speak to us in our hearts, to cultivate love's intimate relationship with us. Only in times of quiet when no one else distracts us, and nothing else draws us away, can Jesus visit us with His love. Let him who wishes to know the presence of Jesus and who desires to enter into bridal love for Jesus keep his times of quiet holy and faithfully for Him.

Jesus is waiting for our love. As important as our sacrifices and our obedience to the commandments are for God (the rich young ruler sacrificed, and kept the commandments), they are not enough. Sacrifices and obedience do not necessarily yield the 'eternal, divine life.' Love does not necessarily pulsate through them. Jesus is pulsating life and love and He wants to impart His nature to us. Therefore, only our love, which stems from the divine, eternal life which He has granted to us, is the proper response to His love for us. This love leads us to keep His commandments, which are His wishes for us. It will lead us to bring Him many gifts, and to offer Him sacrifices—but in a different spirit.

...Bridal love for Jesus is filled with delight. There is no greater, happier, higher, richer love.

(Basilea Schlink, "Bridal Love" © 2001 The Watchword. 3 Jan. 2002
<http://www.watchword.org/schlink/ww29d.html>)

He is waiting for us. He wants us to be close to Him.
He wants to speak to us in our hearts, to cultivate love's
intimate relationship with us.

Day: _____ Date: _____ Time: _____ Location: _____

Manipulation

When you see a woman going after the guys, you probably don't immediately say, "Yes, I see that she really is insecure!" Insecurity dwells in the heart. What you see outwardly is a woman's age-old ability to manipulate and maneuver. When a woman manipulates a situation, she feels personal satisfaction because she believes she is in control.

…

Manipulation and maneuvering can also take the form of serving as a "surrogate (substitute) helpmeet." Many women want to marry as badly as they want to go to Heaven. They long to care for a man, so they run around trying to find at least a "generic" version of the real thing. These precious (but deceived) women constantly look for a man with a need and pounce on that need in hopes of eventually winning the affection of man. Any male in need irresistibly attracts them.

…Women may find more pleasure doing for a man than a woman because the potential "payoff" seems more valuable. She envisions surrendering her "surrogate" apron for an engagement ring.…

…Allow God to use you to minister to brothers and sisters equally with no ulterior motives.

_____

_____

_____

_____

_____

_____

_____

_____

_____

_____

_____

_____

_____

_____

_____

_____

_____

_____

_____

_____

_____

_____

_____

_____

When a woman manipulates a situation, she feels personal
satisfaction because she believes she is in control.

Day: _____ Date: _____ Time: _____ Location: _____

Pre-Romantic Stress Disorder

You have just returned home from a great singles retreat where you once again surrendered your frustration as a single in exchange for God's peace and contentment. As you listen to your answering machine, you hear a certain voice. The most sought-after bachelor you know asks you for a date next weekend. Do you remain calm and give your expectations to the Lord? Or do you jump back in your car and head to the mall to register your china and look at some wedding gowns? Would the prospect of a date with the most eligible bachelor in town cause you to experience the "Pre-romantic Stress Disorder"? Or would you surrender your expectations to Jesus?

For a single woman to experience genuine contentment while soloing in a "couple's world," she must avoid the ditches of discontentment. She needs to learn the mystery of contentment and its power over the restless torture of her desire.

...

Circumstantially, Ruth had the perfect excuse to be discontented. Widowed at a young age, her circumstances provided the perfect breeding ground for self-pity and bitterness....Yet Ruth chose to cling to the God of Israel, whom she found to be trustworthy even in difficult circumstances.

_____

_____

_____

_____

_____

_____

_____

_____

_____

_____

_____

_____

_____

_____

_____

_____

_____

_____

_____

_____

_____

_____

_____

_____

Would the prospect of a date with the most eligible
bachelor in town cause you to experience the
"Pre-romantic Stress Disorder"?

Day: _____ Date: _____ Time: _____ Location: _____

Julian of Norwich

Julian is the most popular of the English mystics. She lived as a Benedictine nun in Norwich, beside the St. Julian Church, from which she most likely took her name. Little is know about Julian's life, although she is mentioned by her contemporary, Margery Kempe.

Julian's book, *Revelations of Divine Love*, entitled her to become the first great female writer in the English language. Despite her disclaimers of being unskilled as an author, she wrote lively prose in a style all her own. She was well trained in the Bible as well as in the teachings of the Church.

Her theology is based upon her mystical experiences. She became ill at the age of 30 and, in the midst of suffering, prayed for a vision of Christ's sufferings. Once in a time of prayer Julian heard the words, "I am the foundation of your praying"—words that greatly influenced her spiritual life. She always pointed to the goodness and love of God, a light in time of darkness for Julian, who lived in an age of social unrest and the fear of the Black Plague.

(Tommy Tenney, *The God Chasers Daily Meditation & Personal Journal* [Shippensburg, Pennsylvania: Destiny Image Publishers, 1999], pp. 80-81)

Revelations of Divine Love

...Oftentimes our trust is not full. We are not sure that God hears us, as we think because of our unworthiness, and because we don't feel right (for we are as barren and dry oftentimes after our prayers as we were before)...For thus have I felt in myself.

And all this brought our Lord suddenly to my mind, and He showed me these words. He said, "I am the Ground of your asking: first it is my will that you have it; and afterwards, I make you to will it; and then, I make you to ask it and you do ask for it. How should it then be that you do not have what you ask for?"

...

For it is most impossible that we should ask mercy and grace, and not have it. For everything that our good Lord makes us to ask, Himself has ordained it to us from without beginning. Here may we see that our asking is not cause of God's goodness; and He showed that in all these sweet words when He said: I am [the] Ground — And our good Lord wills that this be known of His lovers in earth; and the more that we know [it] the more should we ask, if it be wisely taken; and so is our Lord's meaning.

(Adapted from Julian of Norwich, *Revelations of Divine Love*, Grace Warrack, ed. [London:Methuen & Co. Ltd., 1901]. Ch. XLI, 14th Revelation. 7 Jan. 2002 <http://www.ccel.org/j/julian/revelations/home.html>)

_____

_____

_____

_____

I am the Ground of your asking: first it is My will that you have it; and afterwards, I make you to will it; and then, I make you to ask it and you do ask for it.

Day: _____ Date: _____ Time: _____ Location: _____

Biblical Dating Standards

What is a Bozo? A Bozo is a guy whose outward appearance is a façade. It is hard to discern who he really is because of the "makeup and costume" he wears. What he appears to be physically, socially, and even spiritually is just a performance. A Bozo is a counterfeit of a Boaz.

It is possible to avoid such a clown. Your standards and convictions will help you recognize the difference....

...As a prerequisite to every date, you should examine your motive.... Some women even give up their biblical convictions in order to get a date with a certain guy.

Have you dated more Bozos than Boazs? If your answer is yes, you may need to develop higher ideals. A very attractive and popular high school girl was challenged to develop a list of biblical dating standards and to put them into practice. She carried a copy of those standards in her wallet for five years. Thus she dated more Boazs than Bozos because her convictions helped her clearly see the type of guys with whom she was relating and ulti-mately dating. Do you carry God's standards for dating in your heart as well as in your wallet?

_____

_____

_____

_____

_____

_____

Some women even give up their biblical convictions in order
to get a date with a certain guy.

Day: _____ Date: _____ Time: _____ Location: _____

Date Fast

Clear standards for dating and relating will guard you against compromise and making wrong choices out of sudden emotion rather than a God-directed will. These guidelines for your dating friendships will keep God as your focus rather than allowing the guy to become the focus (idol). Clear standards coupled with accountability to a sister in Christ will help you walk in the convictions you establish. To guard you against haphazard meetings or just the "WFs" (weird feelings) in your heart, you need standards for which you will be accountable.

...The issue of standards is most relevant, but may seem simplistic. We acknowledge that some women find it difficult to raise their standards and change their patterns because they are still entangled in the past. Unresolved conflicts with a father, a brother, or an ex-boyfriend may overshadow and control the attraction to Bozos. In this case we suggest a possible date fast, a period of time during which you refrain from accepting another date until you can sort out some of the unresolved conflicts from the past....During the "date fast," [you ~~will~~ can] find time to search for new ways of relating and dating biblically.

_____

_____

_____

_____

_____

_____

_____

_____

_____

_____

_____

_____

_____

_____

_____

_____

_____

_____

_____

_____

_____

_____

_____

_____

_____

During the "date fast," [you ~~will~~ can] find time to search for new ways of relating and dating biblically.

Day: _____ Date: _____ Time: _____ Location: _____

Missionary Dating

"Here comes the bride all dressed in...chains!" Hey, wasn't that supposed to be "all dressed in white"? The last word in the chorus was changed to "chains," not because the bride is marrying a member of a motorcycle gang, but because she made the unwise choice of marrying an unbeliever. The chains symbolize what she has to look forward to as a believer married to an unbeliever. The Word of God speaks clearly about a partnership with an unbeliever....

...

When a single woman experiences a prolonged period of datelessness, loneliness tempts her to compromise her conviction concerning dating a growing Christian. Her dateless state may pressure her to surrender to the temptation of dating an unbeliever. She may justify such a date in the guise of being a witness for Jesus. Many single women have been trapped emotionally with an unbeliever when it all began with "missionary dating." Ponder this: Every unbelieving marriage partner arrived as an unbeliever on the first date. As trite as it may seem, every date is a potential mate. Avoid dating an unbeliever.

...You must set a higher standard and resist dating a guy who is not growing in his intimacy with Christ.

_____

_____

_____

_____

_____

_____

_____

_____

_____

_____

_____

_____

_____

_____

_____

_____

_____

_____

_____

_____

_____

_____

Every unbelieving marriage partner arrived as
an unbeliever on the first date.

Day: _____ Date: _____ Time: _____ Location: _____

Marriage is Not a Dream

Realizing that marriage is not a dream but real life can also help you to wait patiently. Instead of merely being envious, get with a godly woman and see the extra load she carries. Look at all she cannot do, instead of the fact that she has a man in her house. Understand that in reality, married life is not constant communication, daily roses, hugs and kisses, breakfast in bed, and sheer bliss. Marriage is every bit as much work as it is wonderful, even in God's way and time. It is good, but don't be deceived into mistaking it for Heaven.

Since no spouse is perfect, learning to live "as one" is not without its tears. Marriage alone is not a cure-all or answer to every heartfelt need. If you think it is, you had better just keep waiting, for that kind of marriage doesn't exist. Although there is a romantic inside every one of us, you must be realistic regarding marriage or the shock could be devastating.

...

Developing patience is hard. Getting married ahead of God's timing is worse. God may not work according to your time schedule, but He does have your best interests in mind.

_____

_____

_____

_____

_____

_____

_____

_____

_____

_____

_____

_____

_____

_____

_____

_____

_____

_____

_____

_____

_____

_____

_____

Although there is a romantic inside every one of us,
you must be realistic regarding marriage
or the shock could be devastating.

Day: _____ Date: _____ Time: _____ Location: _____

Breaking Your Alabaster Box

What is in your alabaster box? Is your box full of fantasies that began as a little girl while you listened to and watched fairy tales about an enchanting couple living happily ever after? Have you been holding on tightly to your alabaster box of dreams, frantically searching for a man worthy of breaking your box? Take your alabaster box to Jesus and break it in His presence, for He is worthy of such honor. Having responded to your heavenly Bridegroom in such a manner, you can wait with confident assurance that, if it be God's will, He will provide you with an earthly bridegroom.

How do you know if you have broken your alabaster box at the feet of Jesus? Such a decision will be reflected in reckless abandonment to the Lordship of Jesus Christ....Take your alabaster box, with your body, soul, and dreams, and entrust them to Jesus. When He is your Lord, you can joyfully walk in the path of life that He has for you.

...Have you broken the valuable alabaster box yet?

_____

_____

_____

_____

_____

_____

_____

_____

_____

_____

_____

_____

_____

_____

_____

_____

_____

_____

_____

_____

_____

_____

How do you know if you have broken
your alabaster box at the feet of Jesus?

Day: _____ Date: _____ Time: _____ Location: _____

Waiting Periods

…Wherever you are, whatever your circumstances may be…be assured that God has not lost your address or your file. He knows exactly where you are and what you need.…

You make the most important decision in life, giving your life to Jesus Christ, "by faith." The second most important decision concerns your life-mate. This decision also demands the element of faith. Waiting for one's life-mate and then saying "I do" to him demands secure faith, like Ruth's faith in the God of Israel.

…Your faith during the "waiting period" pleases God.

Don't fear or resent the waiting periods in your life. These are the very gardens where the seeds of faith blossom.…

This intruding anxiety about your lack of a life-mate is not reality, but rather a weakness that the Greater Reality is capable of handling. Just go to Jesus as soon as the intruder arrives. Such a practice will only enhance your life as a Lady of Faith. Many single women have not recognized that the trying, frustrating waiting period is the perfect classroom for the Lady of Faith. Don't skip class! Embrace those dateless nights and, by faith, rest in His faithfulness.

_____

_____

_____

_____

_____

_____

_____

_____

_____

_____

_____

_____

_____

_____

_____

_____

_____

_____

_____

_____

_____

_____

_____

_____

_____

_____

_____

_____

_____

Your faith during the "waiting period" pleases God.

Day: _____ Date: _____ Time: _____ Location: _____

Cleanup Time

If you are to know God intimately, then you must seek Him, not only with a whole heart, but also with a clean heart. When you think of the word *bride*, you probably first imagine a beautiful, clean, pure woman in white. No grime or dirt mars the image of purity. As a Christian you are part of the Bride of Christ. Any grime or dirt of sin will mar your image before Him.

The Lord's fiancé must have a clean heart. You must clean up any blot of sin that may arise between you and your heavenly Sweetheart. Sin…is disgusting to Him; He will not abide with it. Picture a couple deeply in love. He loves to be near her—so near he can breathe the fresh aroma of her sweet breath!…What do you think she does before she sees him if she has eaten onions?…Not only does she brush, but she also "Scopes, Close-ups and Gleems." She doesn't want to offend her love!… Sin is far more repulsive to God than even onion breath…. If you want your devotion to God to be complete, don't merely brush at sin lightly. Get in there and confess it, clean it up, and clear it out.

_____

_____

_____

_____

_____

_____

_____

_____

_____

_____

_____

_____

_____

_____

_____

_____

_____

_____

_____

_____

_____

_____

_____

_____

_____

_____

_____

If you want your devotion to God to be complete,
don't merely brush at sin lightly.

Day: _____ Date: _____ Time: _____ Location: _____

Madame Jeanne Guyon

Madame Jeanne Guyon was born at Montargis, France. When she was only 15, she married an invalid who was 38 years old. Unhappy in her marriage, she sought happiness in her devotional life. She lived in a convent under royal order for a year and then was imprisoned in Vincennes and the Bastille because of her religious beliefs. Almost 25 years of her life were spent in confinement. Many of her books were written during that period.

Writing that compels the reader to move into a living experience of Jesus Christ is Madame Guyon's great contribution to devotional literature. *Experiencing the Depths of Jesus Christ* (sometimes entitled *A Short and Very Easy Method of Prayer*) has had a wide influence: Watchman Nee saw that it was translated into Chinese and made available to every new convert in the Little Flock; Francois Fénelon, John Wesley, and Hudson Taylor all highly recommended it to the believers of their day.

(Tommy Tenney, *The God Chasers Daily Meditation & Personal Journal*
[Shippensburg, Pennsylvania: Fresh Bread, 1999], pp. 114-115)

The Effectual Touch in the Will

The Soul then receives an effectual Touch in the Will, which invites it to recollection, and instructs it that God is within, and must be sought there; that He is present in the Heart, and must be there enjoyed.

This discovery, in the beginning, is the source of very great joy to the Soul, as it is an intimation or pledge of happiness to come; in its very commencement; the road it is to pursue is opened and is shown to be that of the Inward Life. This knowledge is the more admirable, as it is the spring of all the Felicity of the Soul, and the solid foundation of interior progress; for those Souls who tend toward God merely by the intellect, even though they should enjoy a some what spiritual contemplation, yet can never enter into Intimate Union, if they do not quit that path and enter this of the Inward Touch, where the whole working is in the Will.

(Madame Jeanne Guyone, *The Way to God*, parapraphs 2 and 3. 3 Jan. 2002
<http://www.passtheword.org/DIALOGS-FROM-THE PAST/waytogod.htm>)

_____

_____

_____

_____

_____

_____

_____

_____

_____

The Soul then receives an effectual Touch in the Will,
which invites it to recollection, and instructs it that God
is within, and must be sought there; that He is present
in the Heart and must be there enjoyed.

Day: _____ Date: _____ Time: _____ Location: _____

Don't Sin Against Yourself

Have you ever been dieting but treated yourself to huge piece of rich chocolate cake with fudge icing to celebrate some special occasion? Cake is good. Cake is desirable. The more cake, the more pleasure. But cake, in the midst of a strict diet, can really make one sick!. The pleasure of a big, luscious piece of cake depends on the right timing, just as the pleasures of sex do.

God also wants to protect you from the sexually transmitted diseases that could affect not only you, but also your future husband....

God also desires to shield you from an unwanted pregnancy. Although precautions exist, pregnancy always remains a possibility. A rushed marriage, adoption, or abortion only complicate the consequences.

God desires to shield you from the negative physical consequences of premarital sex. He wants to protect you from sinning against your body. First Corinthians 6:18 (NIV) says, "Flee from sexual immorality. All other sins a [woman] commits are outside [her] body, but [she] who sins sexually sins against [her] own body." "He wants you to be free from an addiction to premarital sex. Passionate physical exchange is a short-lived high. As with drugs, you keep wanting more intense highs."*

*Tim Stanford, "The Best of Sex," *Campus Life Magazine*, February, 1992, pp. 25-26, as cited in *Lady In Waiting*.

_____

_____

_____

_____

_____

_____

_____

_____

_____

_____

_____

_____

_____

_____

_____

_____

_____

_____

_____

_____

_____

_____

_____

. . . cake, in the midst of a strict diet, can really make one sick!.

Day: _____ Date: _____ Time: _____ Location: _____

Spiritual Pain

Passion makes it difficult to see that God also set physical limits to protect you spiritually. Hebrews 13:4 (NIV) very clearly says that "marriage should be honored by all, and the marriage bed kept pure, for God will judge the adulterer and all the sexually immoral." God judges the sin of immorality. It feels awful to be separated from your Lord by the guilt of sin.

Actions speak louder than words, and this is especially true regarding premarital sex. It is difficult to share Christ with one who knows your reputation. Your actions can also cause weaker brothers and sisters to stumble. One night of passion can totally destroy a reputation you have built over a lifetime. "The spiritual side of sex is often overlooked. Even many Christians are not aware of the profoundly spiritual nature of their sex lives. A person will feel acute spiritual pain and separation from God when engaging in sex outside of marriage, but may not even realize how spiritually beneficial and unifying sex is within marriage."*

God does not intend to deny you pleasure. He protects you so you might enjoy physical health, emotional stability, relational intimacy, and spiritual blessings.

*Tim Stanford, "The Best of Sex," *Campus Life Magazine*, February, 1992, pp. 25-26, as cited in *Lady In Waiting*.

_____

_____

_____

_____

_____

_____

_____

_____

_____

_____

_____

_____

_____

_____

_____

_____

_____

_____

_____

_____

_____

_____

_____

_____

_____

_____

It feels awful to be separated from your Lord by the guilt of sin.

Day: _____ Date: _____ Time: _____ Location: _____

Your Assignment: Wait

Naomi told [Ruth] that Boaz was a candidate for being their kinsman-redeemer.... This simply meant that the Mosaic Law allowed Boaz, as the closest kin, to redeem the childless widow and keep the family name alive....

Naomi instructs Ruth to approach Boaz and ask him if he would be their kinsman-redeemer...His willingness was directly related to the character he had noticed in her responses to life and God.

...

Naomi's response to Boaz's willingness may have put a damper on most single women's racing heartbeat. "Then Naomi said, 'Wait, my daughter, until you find out what happens. For the man will not rest until the matter is settled today' " (Ruth 3:18 NIV). Who has to *wait*? The woman must wait. Who is the one who will not rest? The man, Boaz, will not rest.

Wait. Such an assignment is not to cause suffering, but prevent it. Women experience so much needless pain when they run ahead of God's format. Naomi knew that there may exist an even closer kinsman who would qualify to redeem her and Ruth....Naomi did not want Ruth's heart to race ahead into disappointment in case the circumstances did not go as assumed.

_____

_____

_____

_____

_____

_____

_____

_____

_____

_____

_____

_____

_____

_____

_____

_____

_____

_____

_____

_____

_____

_____

Wait. Such an assignment is not to
cause suffering, but prevent it.

Day: _____ Date: _____ Time: _____ Location: _____

Hannah Smith

Hannah Smith is the author of the popular classic, *The Christian's Secret of a Happy Life*, which was published in 1875. Its spiritual secrets of walking with God have been a great source of spiritual strength to many generations....

The search for God finds its greatest hope as we look within, deep into our spirit, where Christ lives. Smith gives us a series of clues for developing our inner life for receiving the "Divine Seed" and preparing our spirit for ultimate union with Christ.

(Tommy Tenney, *Mary's Prayers and Martha's Recipes* [Shippensburg, Pennsylvania: Fresh Bread, 2002], p. 21)

You Must Move In

A large part of the pain of life comes from the haunting 'fear of evil' which so often besets us. Our lives are full of supposes. Suppose this should happen, or suppose that should happen; what could we do; how could we bear it? But, if we are living in the 'high tower' of the dwelling place of God, all these supposes will drop out of our lives. We shall be 'quiet from the fear of evil,' for no threatenings of evil can penetrate into the 'high tower' of God. Even when walking through the valley of the shadow of death, the psalmist could say 'I will fear no evil'; and, if we are dwelling in God, we can say so too.

But you may ask here how you are to get into this divine dwelling place. To this I answer that you must simply move in. If a house should be taken for us by a friend, and we were told it was ready, and that the lease and all the necessary papers were duly attested and signed, we should not ask how we could get into it ——we should just pack up and move in. And we must do the same here. God says that He is our dwelling place, and the Bible contains all the necessary papers, duly attested and signed. And our Lord invites us, nay more, commands us to enter in and abide there. In effect He says, 'God is your dwelling place, and you must see to it that you take up your abode there. You must move in.'

(Hannah Smith, *The God of All Comfort*, Ch. 8 3 Jan. 2002
<http://www.ccel.org/s/smith_hw/comfort/htm/VIII.htm#VIII

"God is your dwelling place, and you must see to it that you take up your abode there. You must move in."

Day: _____ Date: _____ Time: _____ Location: _____

The Umpire Has the Final Word

...Your lack of contentment is because of *pride*. Pride can be described as an excessively high opinion of what one deserves. When a single's life is not moving in the direction she wants (husband, career children, house, etc.), the arguing often begins. With whom is the single woman arguing? It is none other than the umpire, the arbitrator: Jesus. "And let the peace of Christ rule [arbitrate, umpire] in your hearts..." (Col. 3:15).

The struggle with the Umpire is not limited to the single women up to bat! Every woman who has descended from Eve must learn to trust the call of her heavenly Umpire. The trouble from the beginning was a woman not listening to the Umpire, but reaching for a life on "her terms." Why would a woman argue with such an all-wise Umpire? "Pride only breeds quarrels" (Prov. 13:10a NIV).

...Exchange your pride for Jesus' strength so you may accept whatever assignment the Umpire has for you from this moment forward. Dating is not a reward or a prize for living for Jesus. A Friday night without a date is often a night of "being spared" by an all-wise Umpire.

_____

_____

_____

_____

_____

_____

_____

_____

_____

_____

_____

_____

_____

_____

_____

_____

_____

_____

_____

_____

_____

_____

_____

_____

_____

_____

_____

Why would a woman argue with such an all-wise Umpire?

Day: _____ Date: _____ Time: _____ Location: _____

Take the Radical Route

Does it seem too unrealistic for a woman of the 90's to set her sights on a knight in shining armor?…A single friend (a modern Ruth) wrote a letter in which she admitted that her high ideals often made her feel like the "Long Ranger." She said, "So often I meet women who don't want to go to the deeper, more radical route of separation from our culture in seeking after God's standards." Do we lower our standards because we seem out of step with all our peers? Does the woman in Proverbs 31 seem obsolete? Maybe for the "cosmopolitan" woman she is obsolete, but not for the Lady of Conviction. God has the best in hand for those who seek Him.

Ruth's choice to wait for God's best resulted in her union with a Boaz rather than a Bozo. Ruth not only married a man who was a "pillar of strength" (Boaz), but she also was blessed by the privilege of bearing a son (Obed) who would be part of the lineage of Jesus Christ. Ruth's wise choices resulted in her experiencing God's overwhelming goodness.

_____

_____

_____

_____

_____

_____

_____

_____

_____

_____

_____

_____

_____

_____

_____

_____

_____

_____

_____

_____

_____

_____

_____

_____

_____

_____

*"...women...don't want to go to the deeper,
more radical route of separation from our culture
in seeking after God's standards."*

Day: _____ Date: _____ Time: _____ Location: _____

No End to the Wait

Take courage, single friend. You are not alone in your wait; neither are you alone in the feelings and struggles you encounter. Many godly women have waited and won. Many women have lost hope and compromised. Wait patiently and win triumphantly the future your Father has planned for you. It will always be designed with you in mind and is worth being patient to discover.

Ruth was a wonderful example of a Lady of Patience. Ruth did not allow her circumstances or lack of male companionship to cause her to be impatient. Instead she concentrated on developing companionship with her heavenly Father and chose to let Him bring a husband to her if He saw fit. Concern over the ticking of her "biological clock" did not make her fearful of the future. Instead she concentrated on being a lady of character, not on getting a man. She took one day at a time, knowing that God was not bound by circumstances nor her age. She used the wait to become the woman God wanted her to be. At the end of this personal preparation God chose to provide her with a husband.

_____

_____

_____

_____

_____

_____

_____

_____

_____

_____

_____

_____

_____

_____

_____

_____

_____

_____

_____

_____

_____

_____

_____

_____

_____

Many godly women have waited and won.
Many women have lost hope and compromised.

Day: _____ Date: _____ Time: _____ Location: _____

Compromise

Marriage to a non-Christian brings pain to the believing wife. As women, we long to be known and loved for all we are. A man who is spiritually dead can never know the very intimate spiritual part of you that is your heart. He would be blind to much of what you would try to share with him. He could never know and understand you fully.

Be careful when you begin to think that you are "in love" and you "just can't live without him." Think again. Think of the loneliness you will feel when your husband will not attend church with you. Think of the angry bickering that may take place between the two of you because he can never understand the depths of your spiritual awareness and, consequently, your convictions. If you do not think about this now, you may one day think, "Before I couldn't live without him; now I can hardly live with him."...

Please consider a greater consequence than being unhappily married to a man who does not know your Lord....Will it be worth the compromise when your children look up at you and ask why daddy doesn't love Jesus?

_____

_____

_____

_____

_____

_____

_____

_____

_____

_____

_____

_____

_____

_____

_____

_____

_____

_____

_____

_____

_____

_____

_____

_____

. . . you may one day think, "Before I couldn't live without him; now I can hardly live with him."

Day: _____ Date: _____ Time: _____ Location: _____

Hannah Smith

A Lesson in the Interior Life

By rejoicing in Him, however, I do not mean rejoicing in ourselves, although I fear most people think this is really what is meant. It is their feelings or their revelations or their experiences that constitute the groundwork of their joy and if none of these are satisfactory they see no possibility of joy at all.

But the lesson the Lord is trying to teach us all the time is the lesson of self-effacement. He commands us to look away from self and all self's experiences, to crucify self and count it dead, to cease to be interested in self, and to know nothing and be interested in nothing but God

The reason for this is that God has destined us for a higher life than the self-life. That just as He has destined the caterpillar to become the butterfly and therefore has appointed the caterpillar life to die, in order that the butterfly life may take its place, so He has appointed our self-life to die in order that the divine life may become ours instead. The caterpillar effaces itself in its grub form, that it may evolve or develop

into its butterfly form. It dies that it may live.
And just so must we.

(Hannah Smith, *The Christian's Secret of a Happy Life* [Christian Witness Co.], Ch. 18. 3 Jan. 2002
<http://www.ccel.org/s/smith_hw/secret/secret21.htm>)

_____

_____

_____

_____

_____

_____

_____

_____

_____

_____

_____

_____

_____

_____

_____

_____

God has destined us for a higher life than the self-life.

Day: _____ Date: _____ Time: _____ Location: _____

Cause and Effect

When you marry, you do not choose blessings or curses for you alone; you choose for the generations after you. If you choose to wait patiently for your knight in shining armor, you will be blessed by the heritage that a prince brings. If you choose to run eagerly ahead of God's plan and marry a man with no conscience toward God, you will reap the life's course he follows, but not alone. Your children's and grandchildren's lives will be directly affected by the man you marry.

…

God warned His people in Deuteronomy of the long-term effect of their choices.…

Deuteronomy 28:2, 15, and 32 show that God has always desired to bless His people, but He will not force them to do what is best. In His Word He has often warned us to wait, to be careful, and to trust Him. He will not make us wait. His heart of love begs us to listen and obey so He may bless us and the dear ones who will one day look to and follow us.…

You must choose to wait patiently for God's best.

_____

_____

_____

_____

_____

_____

_____

_____

_____

_____

_____

_____

_____

_____

_____

_____

_____

_____

_____

_____

_____

_____

_____

_____

_____

You must choose to wait patiently for God's best.

Day: _____ Date: _____ Time: _____ Location: _____

Single Hours

The perfect time to make the most of every opportunity is while you are single. Every believer should use time wisely as Ephesians 5:15-17 (NIV) says....

Rather than staying home worrying about another "dateless" Saturday night, realize how much valuable time has been entrusted to you at this point in your life. Rather than resent your many single hours, embrace them as a gift from God—a package that contains opportunities to serve Him that are limited only by your own self-pity and lack of obedience.

...Countless single women stay home rather than travel alone into the unknown. They not only miss out on being encouraged by others, but also are not exposed to new relationships when they remain at home tied up by cords of fear and feeling sorry for themselves.

If a single woman allows the fearful prospect of meeting new people and new challenges to keep her at home, she may find herself bored and lonely while all the time missing many satisfying and fulfilling experiences....

Are you busy serving Jesus during your free time, or do you waste hours trying to pursue and snag an available guy?

_____

_____

_____

_____

_____

_____

_____

_____

_____

_____

_____

_____

_____

_____

_____

_____

_____

_____

_____

_____

_____

_____

_____

Rather than resent your many single hours,
embrace them as a gift from God...

Day: _____ Date: _____ Time: _____ Location: _____

Madame Guyon

The Prayer of the Heart

Let all pray; you should live by prayer, as you should live by love. "I counsel you to buy of me gold tried in the fire, that ye may be rich." (Rev. iii. 18.) This is very easily obtained, much more easily than you can conceive.

Come all ye that are athirst to the living waters, nor lose your precious moments in hewing out cisterns that will hold no water. (John vii. 37; Jer. ii. 1 .) Come ye famishing souls, who find nought to satisfy you; come, and ye shall be filled! Come, ye poor afflicted ones, bending beneath your load of wretchedness and pain, and ye shall be consoled! Come, ye sick, to your physician, and be not fearful of approaching him because ye are filled with diseases; show them, and they shall be healed!

Children, draw near to your Father, and he will embrace you in the arms of love! Come ye poor, stray, wandering sheep, return to your Shepherd! Come, sinners, to your Saviour! Come ye dull, ignorant, and illiterate, ye who think yourselves the most incapable of prayer! ye are more peculiarly called and adapted thereto. Let

all without exception come, for Jesus Christ
hath called ALL.

(Madame Jeanne Guyon, *A Short & Very Easy Method of Prayer*, Ch. I. 3 Jan .2002
<http://www.passtheword.org/DIALOGS-FROM-THE-PAST/methodofprayer.htm>)

_____

_____

_____

_____

_____

_____

_____

_____

_____

_____

_____

_____

_____

_____

*Children, draw near to your Father, and he will embrace you
in the arms of love! Come ye poor, stray, wandering sheep,
return to your Shepherd!*

Day: _____ Date: _____ Time: _____ Location: _____

Prayer Partners

Do you have a prayer partner? Or do you only have someone with whom you have regular pity parties? If you do not have a prayer partner, ask the Lord right now for such a gift. A prayer partner can help you pray for others....

...Praying regularly with someone (or a small group) is such a vital part of your service to God. To intercede on behalf of someone else's need is a privilege. When you intercede with a partner, the "duet" of harmony before God can change your world. Matthew 18:19 (NIV) describes this harmonious duet: "Again, I tell you that if two of you on earth agree about anything you ask for; it will be done for you by My Father in heaven." That little verb *agree* refers to harmony. Do you have someone with whom you can prayerfully approach God in harmony? Rather than searching for a life-partner, look for a prayer partner. Together you can participate in God-given prayer projects. Together you can discover how you can take your concerns for others and turn them into prayer projects.

_____

_____

_____

_____

_____

_____

_____

_____

_____

_____

_____

_____

_____

_____

_____

_____

_____

_____

_____

_____

_____

_____

_____

_____

_____

_____

When you intercede with a partner, the "duet" of harmony
before God can change your world.

Day: _____ Date: _____ Time: _____ Location: _____

Madame Guyon

Meditative Reading

There are two ways of introducing a soul into prayer, which should be pursued for some time; the one is meditation, the other is reading accompanied by meditation.

Meditative reading is the choosing some important practical or speculative truth, always preferring the practical, and proceeding thus: whatever truth you have chosen, read only a small portion of it, endeavoring to taste and digest it; to extract the essence and substance of it, and proceed no farther while any savor or relish remains in the passage: then take up your book again, and proceed as before, seldom reading more than half a page at a time.

It is not the quantity that is read, but the manner of reading that yields us profit. Those who read fast, reap no more advantage, than a bee would by only skimming over the surface of the flower, instead of waiting to penetrate into it, and extract its sweets. Much reading is rather for scholastic subjects, than divine truths; to receive profit from spiritual books, we must read as I have described; and I am certain that if that method were pursued, we should become gradually habituated to prayer by our reading and more fully disposed for its exercise.

(Madame Jeanne Guyon, *A Short & Very Easy Method of Prayer*, Ch. II. 3 Jan .2002 <http://www.passtheword.org/DIALOGS-FROM-THE-PAST/methodofprayer.htm>)

It is not the quantity that is read,
but the manner of reading, that yields us profit.

Day: _____ Date: _____ Time: _____ Location: _____

Spiritual Eye Wash

In order to have "eyes of faith," you may have to use a spiritual eye wash to remove the debris that the enemy has dropped into your eyes. The Lady of Faith will have times when her secure eyes of faith begin to blink into an anxious twitch of insecure, sensual sight. She can admit her insecurity to her heavenly Fiancé and He can calm the twitching eyes. Spending some quality time in the Word is the best "eye wash" for "eyes of faith."

…A Lady of Faith…can only be content in this trying situation if she has her "eyes of faith" properly focused on the ultimate relationship—with her heavenly Bridegroom. Datelessness is a common type of debris that irritates the "eyes of faith," but the eye wash treatment—quality time with Jesus and reading His Word—is always effective.

…

One young lady faithfully attended her church for years. Often she needed reminding that "he's just not here yet." God brought her Boaz from across the country to where she was in Florida….Many tears of faith had washed away the debris that often caused her to doubt if she would ever get married.

_____

_____

_____

_____

_____

_____

_____

_____

_____

_____

_____

_____

_____

_____

_____

_____

_____

_____

_____

_____

_____

_____

_____

_____

Spending some quality time in the Word is the best
"eye wash" for "eyes of faith."

Day: _____ Date: _____ Time: _____ Location: _____

Devotion

…It is hard enough for a single woman to keep her focus where it should be without friends making insensitive comments [about not being married]. How much better it would be for the Lady in Waiting if she were encouraged to pursue her undistracted devotion to the Lord Jesus Christ, instead of being made to feel like she does not quite measure up.…

Much too often people view a single woman as though she should be pitied rather than envied. Nothing could be further from the truth. A Lady in Waiting had the advantage of being able to develop her love relationship with Christ without the distraction that a husband or family inherently bring to one's heart.

This has been God's plan from the beginning. He tenderly created woman to love Him and to experience the blessedness of fellowship with Him. In those first days, Eve communed with God in indescribable fellowship and oneness. When God came to walk in the cool of the day, there was no fear; only love. Eve had only positive feelings about God. She loved Him and knew He loved her. She enjoyed Him and devoted herself totally to His pleasure.

_____

_____

_____

_____

_____

_____

_____
_____
_____
_____
_____
_____
_____
_____
_____
_____
_____
_____
_____
_____
_____
_____
_____
_____
_____
_____

A Lady in Waiting had the advantage of being able to develop her love relationship with Christ without the distraction ...

Day: _Mon._ Date: _12/29/08_ Time: _12:40pm_ Location: _home_

Amy Carmichael

Amy Carmichael was born December 16, 1867, in Millisle, Northern Ireland, the oldest of three sisters and four brothers. She was raised in the Presbyterian church.

During her adolescence Amy showed signs of a great poetic gift. In 1885 she had a mystical experience that set the course of her spiritual pursuit.

Amy's passion for missions was ignited in 1887 when she heard China Inland Mission founder Hudson Taylor speak. Five years later, God's words "Go ye" were all the confirmation she needed to set her course for foreign lands. She was rejected by C.I.M. because of her frail health, but in 1893 she served the Japanese mission as a "Keswick missionary," and in 1895 she departed for India. Miss Carmichael soon formed the evangelizing "Woman's Band" and took in her first "refugee."

In 1900 she moved to the infamous Dohnavur where she eventually founded the "Dohnavur Fellowship." In 1903 Amy's *Things as They Are* was published, launching her career as a prolific writer. In 1916 she founded "Sisters of Common Life," a spiritual support group.

Miss Carmichael was crippled by a fall in 1931; four years later, she became bedridden. She remained thus until her death on January 18, 1951, and was buried at her beloved Dohnavur.

(<www.heroesofhistory.com/page49.html> as cited in Tommy Tenney, *Mary's Prayers and Martha's Recipes* [Shippensburg, Pennsylvania: Fresh Bread, 2002], pp. 13-14)

Distractions in Prayer

Sometimes nothing helps so much as to turn from trying to pray and instead, to read on the knees of the spirit some familiar passage from the Bible, for those words have a power in them to effect that of which they speak. Another sure way into peace is found in a literal obedience to Colossians 3:16. Turn a psalm or a hymn into prayer, read or repeat it aloud, for to speak to oneself deep down in one's heart, using words that one knows and loves, is often a wonderfully quickening thing to do, and nothing more quickly and gently leads one into the place of peace, where prayer is born...

Sometimes we cannot find words... do not be afraid of silence in your prayer time. It may be that you are meant to listen, not to speak. So wait before the Lord. Wait in stillness... And in that stillness, assurance will come to you..... You will know that you are heard; you will know that your Lord ponders the voice of your humble desires; you will hear quiet words spoken to you yourself, perhaps to your grateful surprise and refreshment.

(Amy Carmichael, *Thou Givest...They Gather* [Fort Washington, Pennsylvania: Christian Literature Crusade, 1958], pp. 45-48, as cited in Tommy Tenney, *Mary's Prayers and Martha's Recipes* [Shippensburg, Pennsylvania: Fresh Bread, 2002], pp. 14-15)

God, I want to hear your quiet words. I want time with you to be special and set apart. Help me to make that time become a reality. I love you.

do not be afraid of silence in your prayer time. It may be that you are meant to listen, not to speak.

Day: _____ Date: _____ Time: _____ Location: _____

What's Your View?

...*"I [Naomi] went out full, but the Lord has brought me back empty.
...the Lord has witnessed against me and the Almighty has afflicted me?' "*
(Ruth 1:21).

Would you be devoted to a God like Naomi's? In Naomi's bitterness, she
no longer referred to God as "the Lord" as she had in verses 8 and 9, but
with a title that can cause one to feel alienated and insignificant—"the
Almighty." Though Ruth clung to Naomi as a mother, she did not accept her
mother-in-law's view of God for herself. ["If we think of Him (God) as cold
and exacting, we shall find it impossible to love Him, and our lives will be
ridden with servile fear."]*

Your past experiences, present circumstances, or your parents' devotion
or lack thereof may cause you to have an incorrect view of God. But nothing and no one can give you a clearer picture of the true God than slipping
under His wings and discovering for yourself Who God really is, the refuge
for which you long. He desires for you to come again "into the garden" and
walk with Him in complete fellowship. This is the fullness of devotion.

*A.W. Tozer, *The Root of the Righteous* (Camp Hill, Pennsylvania: Christian Publishing, Inc. 1985),
p. 5, as cited in *Lady In Waiting*.

_____

_____

_____

_____

_____

_____

...nothing and no one can give you a clearer picture of the true God than slipping under His wings and discovering for yourself Who God really is...

Day: _____ Date: _____ Time: _____ Location: _____

Maximizing Fellowship With God

As a single, you have a wonderful opportunity to use your time to max-imize your fellowship with God. When you love someone, you give them your heart, the center of your being. God asks for no less. He desires a total-ly devoted heart. Deuteronomy 6:5 says that you are to love Him with all your heart (deepest devotion), your soul (what you think and what you feel), and your might (your strength and energy).

Many women today are devoted, all right! They have devoted themselves to developing a love relationship, but not with the Lord. They erroneously seek for love in sensations and promises. The world's version of love is something they want to "fall into." Meanwhile, "true love" escapes them. True loves can only be found in undistracted devotion to Jesus Christ.

To love Him like this, you must know Him intimately....It is a personal, intimate knowledge. Do you have a devotion to God that causes people to marvel at how intimately you know Him? Do you know God in a way that causes Him to be an intimate, personal part of your being as you may desire a husband to one day be?

_____

_____

_____

_____

_____

_____

_____

_____

_____

_____

_____

_____

_____

_____

_____

_____

_____

_____

_____

_____

_____

_____

_____

_____

_____

_____

As a single, you have a wonderful opportunity to use your time to maximize your fellowship with God.

Day: _____ Date: _____ Time: _____ Location: _____

Contentment

Whether married or single,…the key to your enjoying this moment deals with your inner contentment.…

…

Whether married or single, one must learn that it is Jesus who strengthens you to walk in the most dismal or delightful of circumstances. True contentment is learned. You are not born with it and you cannot buy it at one of K-Mart's blue-light specials. Your classroom for learning is your daily life. Every shattered dream or unfulfilled expectation serves as a perfect opportunity to learn contentment. These circumstances are your classroom assignments for learning the mystery of contentment. Learning contentment will require complete dependence upon Jesus, for difficult circumstances without the strength of Jesus can rob you of potential contentment. Do not be deceived into thinking you do not need Jesus' strength to face the good circumstances as well as the bad. When the sun is shining with no clouds in sight, you may assume that you can securely bask in the sunshine without any prospect of rain; however, this full feeling can easily breed a tendency to ignore Jesus. "Otherwise, I may have too much and disown you and say, 'Who is the Lord?' " (Prov. 30:9a NIV)

_____

_____

_____

_____

_____

_____

_____

_____

_____

_____

_____

_____

_____

_____

_____

_____

_____

_____

_____

_____

_____

_____

_____

_____

_____

Every shattered dream or unfulfilled expectation serves as a
perfect opportunity to learn contentment.

Day: _____ Date: _____ Time: _____ Location: _____

The Place of Rest

You don't know what tomorrow holds, but you do know who holds tomorrow. Say this with the psalmist:

O Lord, my heart is not proud, nor my eyes haughty; nor do I involved myself in great matters, or in things too difficult for me. Surely I have composed and quieted my soul; like a weaned child rests against his mother, my soul is like a weaned child within me. O [substitute your name], hope in the Lord from this time forth and forever (Psalm 131).

The place of rest that the psalmist found was a result of the choice he made. This quietness of soul did not come naturally to him. He actively chose to take himself out of involvement and quiet his soul (his mind, will, and emotions). He chose to put his hope in God. Are you trying to involve yourself in matters that are too great for you? Can you see into a man's heart? Can you know the future? You know Someone who does know men's hearts and the future. Patiently rest against His chest. He will bring you the peace you need....By an act of your will you must choose to trust God regardless of what happens.

_____

_____

_____

_____

_____

_____

_____

_____

_____

_____

_____

_____

_____

_____

_____

_____

_____

_____

_____

_____

_____

_____

_____

_____

*By an act of your will you must choose to trust God
regardless of what happens.*

Day: _____ Date: _____ Time: _____ Location: _____

Madame Guyon

Prayer Divinely Explained

Prayer is the effusion of the heart in the presence of God; "I have poured out my soul before the Lord," said the mother of Samuel. (1 Sam. i. 15.) The prayer of the wise men at the feet of Christ in the stable of Bethlehem, was signified by the incense they offered

Prayer is a certain warmth of love, melting dissolving and sublimating the soul, and causing it to ascend unto God, and, as the soul is melted, odors rise from it; and these sweet exhalations proceed from the consuming fire of love within.

This is illustrated in the Canticles, [Song of Solomon] i. 12, where the spouse says, "While the king sitteth at his table, my spikenard sendeth forth the smell thereof." The table is the centre of the soul; and when God is there, and we know how to dwell near, and abide with Him, the sacred presence gradually dissolves the hardness of the soul, and, as it melts, fragrance issues forth; hence it is, that the Beloved says of his spouse, in seeing her soul melt when he spoke, "Who is this that cometh out of the wilderness, like pillars of smoke perfumed with myrrh and frankincense?' (Cant. [Song of Solomon] v. 6; iii. 6.)

(Madame Jeanne Guyone, *A Short & Very Easy Method of Prayer*, Ch. XX. 3 Jan. 2002
<http://www.passtheword.org/DIALOGS-FROM-THE-PAST/methodofprayer.htm>)

_____

_____

_____

_____

_____

_____

_____

_____

_____

_____

_____

_____

_____

_____

_____

_____

_____

Prayer is the effusion of the heart in the presence of God.

Day: _____ Date: _____ Time: _____ Location: _____

Consider... Your Friends

When Ruth told Naomi, "your people shall be my people," she understood that she would not be able to grow closer to the God of Israel if she remained among the Moabites (her own people). Ironically, God called Moab His washbasin (see Ps. 60:8; 108:9). One rinses dirt off in a washbasin. Ruth chose to leave the washbasin and head for Bethlehem which means the "house of bread."*

Even today there exist "Moabites" who will undermine your growth if you spend too much time with them....Realizing that one's friends drive you either toward or away from God, you may need to find a "new people" who will encourage your growth and not hinder it....

...When a woman stops growing spiritually, the lack of progress can often be traced back to a friendship that undermined her commitment to Jesus.

Take a moment to think about the spiritual depth of the girlfriend who influences you the most. Is she daily becoming all that Jesus desires? If so, her growth will challenge you to grow. On the other hand, her apathy may ultimately be contagious.

*Scofield Bible (New York: Oxford University Press, 1967), p. 51, as cited in *Lady In Waiting*.

_____

_____

_____

_____

_____

...one's friends drive you either toward or away from God...

 *Lady In Waiting*

Day: _____ Date: _____ Time: _____ Location: _____

Behavior Patterns

Part of reckless abandonment is realizing how much our culture has affected our behavior patterns. You want to be Christlike, but your life *style* is a reflection of *Vogue* magazine or *Cosmopolitan* rather a new creation in Christ. A.W. Tozer said, "A whole new generation of Christians has come up believing that it is possible to 'accept' Christ without forsaking the world."* Ruth had to forsake the familiar and comfortable in order to receive God's best for her life.

...

One single was persecuted, not by non-Christians but by Christians, because she chose to spend her summer studying at a Bible Institute rather than playing in the sunshine with her friends. They actually accused her of thinking she was better than them because she planned to study the Bible intensively for eight weeks. Unfortunately, our self-centered culture in America has penetrated the Church so much that a young woman not only has to choose against the American culture, but sometimes against the more subtle, worldly Christian subculture tainting the Body of Christ.

*A.W. Tozer, *The Pursuit of God*. (Camp Hill, Pennsylvania: Christian Publishing, Inc., 1982), p. 16, as cited in *Lady In Waiting*.

_____

_____

_____

_____

_____

_____

_____

_____

_____

_____

_____

_____

_____

_____

_____

_____

_____

Part of reckless abandonment is realizing
how much our culture has affected our behavior patterns.

Day: _____ Date: _____ Time: _____ Location: _____

Imitations

There are many imitations of a true pearl, but with years, the shiny pearl paint cracks and wears off and all that is left is an unattractive bead hanging on a string. God's Spirit, however, produces true inner beauty, as you confess your sin, avoid displeasing God's Spirit, obey even the slightest of His promptings, and give the Holy Spirit full control of your life. Pearls of godly character take time to develop, but how blessed is the woman adorned by them.

You can settle for an imitation necklace of fake pearls by trying to simply cover over ungodly character, or you can allow the Holy Spirit to use the sands of singleness to create the real thing. If you want a cheap imitation, a modeling or charm school will be sufficient for what you seek. But if you want genuine pearls, you must allow the Holy Spirit to perform a special work in your life. Determine to string lovely pearl "necklace of virtue" as a treasure for your Lord.

*"Providing lasting pleasure
potential beyond measure,
the rarest of treasure,
a reputation of virtuous character."
—JMK*

_____

_____

_____

_____

_____

_____

_____

_____

_____

_____

_____

_____

_____

_____

_____

_____

_____

_____

_____

_____

_____

_____

_____

*... if you want genuine pearls, you must allow the Holy
Spirit to perform a special work in your life.*

Day: _____ Date: _____ Time: _____ Location: _____

The Mom Maneuver

Another form of maneuvering is to become the guy's "mom." Insecure females all too often deceive themselves into thinking that because they do so much for a particular young man, they will surely win his love. *Wrong!* It is easy for a man, whether he is young or old, to let a woman sacrifice for him. Why? Most men are used to the sacrifices of a woman. Good ol' mom has been sacrificing for him since the womb. Sure, the young man will say, "Thanks," but young men do not marry their mothers! When a woman does something nice for a certain guy, he usually does not spend the rest of the day thinking about her unselfish service (he may be accustomed to receiving). The woman may begin to feel used.

Some women prepare meals, sew on buttons, and wash the guy's clothes—all the things a mom would do—assuming all this is practice for their future together. Inevitably, the man she has served so unselfishly may fall for a girl who can't bake or sew and thinks you take all the clothes to the dry cleaners that "fluff and fold."

_____

_____

_____

_____

_____

_____

_____

_____

_____

_____

_____

_____

_____

_____

_____

_____

_____

_____

_____

_____

_____

_____

_____

_____

_____

Most men are used to the sacrifices of a woman.

Day: _____ Date: _____ Time: _____ Location: _____

Man Hunt

To quit the hunt and stop "going after the guys," you must first avoid maneuvering and manipulating. Ruth did, and God can give you the grace to do it too. Believe that God will take care of you regardless of your circumstances. Don't put your own devices to work. You can only see the outward man from today's perspective. God sees men's hearts from the perspective of eternity. With His perspective, He can see much better what you need. Trust Him and let Him show you His dependable love for you.

Second, you must put your security in Christ. He longs for you to be secure in His love. He wants to protect, lead, and love you. To develop security, give your heart and emotions to the Lord....

...To build security into your life, spend time in God's Word....

By spending time in God's Word, you will also learn what God thinks of you....

You are very special to God—so special that He has plans for you....

Do not allow insecurity to motivate you to maneuver or manipulate your relationships. Instead of hunting for a husband or boyfriend, concentrate on becoming a woman of excellence....

_____

_____

_____

_____

_____

_____

_____

_____

_____

_____

_____

_____

_____

_____

_____

_____

_____

_____

_____

_____

_____

_____

Instead of hunting for a husband or boyfriend,
concentrate on becoming a woman of excellence....

Day: _____ Date: _____ Time: _____ Location: _____

Julian of Norwich

Loved of God

For as the body is clad in the cloth, and the flesh in the skin, and the bones in the flesh, and the heart in the whole, so are we, soul and body, clad in the Goodness of God, and enclosed. Yea, and more homely: for all these may waste and wear away but the Goodness of God is ever whole; and more near to us, without any likeness; for truly our Lover desireth that our soul cleave to Him with all its might, and that we be evermore cleaving to His Goodness. For of all things that heart may think, this pleaseth most God, and soonest speedeth the soul.

For our soul is so specially loved of Him that is highest, that it overpasseth the knowing of all creatures: that is to say there is no creature that is made that may fully know how much and how sweetly and how tenderly our Maker loveth us. And therefore we may with grace and His help stand in spiritual beholding, with everlasting marvel of this high, overpassing inestimable Love that Almighty God hath to us of His Goodness. And therefore we may ask of our Lover with reverence all that we will.

For our natural Will is to have God, and the Good Will of God is to have us; and we may never cease from willing nor from longing till we have Him in fullness of joy: and then may we no more desire.

For He willeth that we be occupied in knowing and loving till the time that we shall be fulfilled in Heaven; and therefore was this lesson of Love shewed, with all that followeth, as ye shall see. For the strength and the Ground of all was shewed in the First Sight. For of all things the beholding and the loving of the Maker maketh the soul to seem less in his own sight; and most filleth him with reverent dread and true meekness; with plenty of charity to his even-Christians.

(Julian of Norwich, *Revelations of Divine Love*. Grace Warrack, ed. [London: Methuen & Co. Ltd., 1901] Ch. VI 7 Jan. 2002 <http://www.ccel.org/j/julian/revelations/revelations.html>)

For as the body is clad in the cloth, and the flesh in the skin, and the bones in the flesh, and the heart in the whole, so are we, soul and body, clad in the Goodness of God.

Day: _____ Date: _____ Time: _____ Location: _____

Sabotage!

...realize that a single woman can sabotage her own contentment by defrauding herself. A single woman can defraud herself as effectively as her male counterpart. Protect your contentment by adopting this "Eleventh Commandment": Thou shalt not defraud thyself.

Women defraud themselves by confusing ministry with matrimony. A guy tries to help a girl grow spiritually, and she sees his care and interest as leading inevitably to marriage. Another guy and girl work on a ministry team together and their spiritual intimacy is confused in her mind with romantic intentions.

Misread intentions between males and females put them on a collision course. The crash can be avoided if the Lady of Contentment would keep in mind that her emotions must be submitted to the facts: ministering together is a privilege as a believer, not an automatic marriage opportunity. Daily, throughout the world, women's hearts are broken because they allow their emotions to run ahead of commitments. Women, young and old, seem to resist controlling their emotions. As a result, they end up emotional cripples, angry at the men who failed to live up to their emotional fantasies.

_____

_____

_____

_____

_____

_____

———————————————————————————————

———————————————————————————————

———————————————————————————————

———————————————————————————————

———————————————————————————————

———————————————————————————————

———————————————————————————————

———————————————————————————————

———————————————————————————————

———————————————————————————————

———————————————————————————————

———————————————————————————————

———————————————————————————————

———————————————————————————————

———————————————————————————————

———————————————————————————————

*...a single woman can sabotage her own contentment
by defrauding herself.*

Day: _____ Date: _____ Time: _____ Location: _____

Reality vs. Fantasy

An important method of limiting your own self-defrauding is through daily discipline over "prenuptial fantasies." Such fantasies may provide you an escape from monotonous reality, but these moments are dangerous. They will aggravate your struggle for contentment because they are not innocent daydreams, but attack on your godly contentment. You may be so used to daily fantasies that you might not even realize when you begin daydreaming again about your prince.

Often a single woman's struggle with contentment can be traced back to her fantasies more than to her frustrating circumstances. Just think for a moment about three words from Second Corinthians 10:5 (KJV): "Casting down imaginations." Fantasizing about a future with guy you have been watching in Sunday school or at work is nothing more than your very active imagination. What should you do when you start daydreaming about a guy you've never dated or even formally met? You must take your thoughts to Jesus and leave them in His capable hands. This daily discipline of taking your fantasies to Jesus is the foundation for your future as a contented woman, whether you are married or single.

_____

_____

_____

_____

_____

_____

_____

_____

_____

_____

_____

_____

_____

_____

_____

_____

_____

_____

_____

_____

_____

_____

_____

_____

_____

_____

_____

You may be so used to daily fantasies that you might not even realize when you begin daydreaming again about your prince.

Day: _____ Date: _____ Time: _____ Location: _____

Jessie Penn-Lewis

The Presence of God

'Oh God when Thou wentest forth before Thy people, when Thou didst march through the wilderness, the earth shook, the heavens also dropped at the Presence of God; even Sinai itself was moved at the Presence of God' (Psalm lxviii. 7-8)

What a glorious ringing shout of triumph there is in these words! They seem to vividly picture the victorious march of an all-conquering King with everything going down before Him. Habakkuk gives us the same conception of the all-victorious Presence of Jehovah. 'Thou didst march through the land for victory with Thine Anointed' (Hab. iii. 13 R.V.)

The manifested Presence of God will alone move the 'Sinais.' How foolish we are to attempt to 'push' them. The walls of Jericho fell down without one single push, yet we seem to think we must do our little best and then God will do the rest. Nay, it is 'stand still and see the salvation of God.' It is the manifested Presence of Jehovah we need; He must march forth before us and the biggest 'Sinai' will be moved before Him.
On the 'Sinais'! How we groan over them! That

Sinai of self, will it never go? That idol we have surrendered so often and yet there it stands still the same! That Sinai in our Christian work, and many others known best to God and ourselves. How we take our little spades, do our little best, push and push, dig and dig failing utterly to make the least impression.

'Oh God...when Thou wentest forth...even Sinai itself...!'

It is the Presence of God we need. How can we obtain His Presence, thus moving so gloriously before us?

We must first be willing for His manifested Presence in us.

(Jessie Penn-Lewis, "The Presence of God," *The Overcomer* [January, 1929], p.1)

_____

_____

_____

_____

_____

_____

It is the manifested Presence of Jehovah we need;
He must march forth before us and the biggest
"Sinai" will be moved before Him.

Day: _____ Date: _____ Time: _____ Location: _____

Wisdom and Grace

How many times a week do you find yourself in a position where some-one has shared a need with you and you want so much to respond with wisdom and grace? Isaiah 50:4 (NIV) says, "The Sovereign Lord has given me an instructed tongue, to know the word that sustains the weary. He wakens me morning by morning, wakens my ear to listen like one being taught." Do you have a hard time responding to such an early wake-up call? Rising early to develop the tongue of a disciple will open a door of ministry to those who are weary, whether they are at work, at church, or even at the grocery store. Your very words will be a ministry of healing and encouragement. "The tongue that brings healing is a tree of life, but a deceitful tongue crushes the spirit" (Prov. 15:4 NIV). Such predawn training will give you the privilege of becoming God's garden hose in a land of many thirsty people.

...

...purchase some pre-stamped postcards and try to send them regularly to different people who need a refreshing word. The Lord wants you to be involved in the lives of those around you....

_____

_____

_____

_____

_____

_____

_____

_____

_____

_____

_____

_____

_____

_____

_____

_____

_____

_____

_____

_____

_____

_____

_____

_____

_____

_____

...predawn training will give you the privilege of becoming
God's garden hose in a land of many thirsty people.

Day: _____ Date: _____ Time: _____ Location: _____

Check Your Heart

If the Lord wants to give you a man, He does not need your clever "chance rendezvous." This is not advocating that you avoid men completely and expect the Lord to "UPS" His choice to your front door. You need to participate in activities that involve men and women, but be sensitive to your motives whenever you find yourself in the presence of "available men." Consider this Scripture whenever checking your motives and your pulse! Proverbs 16:2 (NIV) says, "All a man's ways seem innocent to him, but motives are weighed by the Lord."

You can prevent disappointing moments if you check your heart whenever you go to a singles' activity. Much preparation (like taking a shower, putting on makeup, styling your hair, doing your nails, and choosing the perfect outfit) precedes one's attending such an activity, yet so little heart preparation does. The gal with sensual sight can become so obsessed with finding her guy that she neglects her inner self. Orpah's style (logical sight) tends to become the norm, but Ruth offers an alternative to this vain search for Mr. Right. She demonstrates what it means to be a Lady of Faith.

_____

_____

_____

_____

_____

_____

_____

_____

_____

_____

_____

_____

_____

_____

_____

_____

_____

_____

_____

_____

_____

_____

_____

_____

_____

_____

You can prevent disappointing moments if you check your heart whenever you go to a singles' activity.

Day: _____ Date: _____ Time: _____ Location: _____

Eyes of Faith

...Ruth certainly must have considered the probability of remaining single if she went with Naomi. Even though it promised no prospects of a husband, she chose to follow Naomi and her God back to Bethlehem. Ruth chose to trust God with her future. She looked not with sensual sight, but through "eyes of faith." Even though Ruth was young in her faith in the God of Israel, she chose to trust with her heart for the future her eyes could not yet see.

...Your hope cannot be put in some dreamed-up future. It must be in the God who knows your past, present, and future, and loves you enough to give you the best.

...

Do you long to please Him? Then reconsider your circumstances and realize that what seems to be a hopeless situation (no prospects on the horizon) is just the flip side of the view through "eyes of faith."

Sometimes in an attempt to be a Lady of Faith, one can get sidetracked trying to hurry the "male order delivery" process.

...God knows when your heart aches for these precious things. But He also knows that these earthly things will not make you secure.

_____

_____

_____

_____

_____

_____

_____

_____

_____

_____

_____

_____

_____

_____

_____

_____

_____

_____

_____

_____

_____

_____

_____

_____

_____

Your hope cannot be put in some dreamed-up future.

Day: _____ Date: _____ Time: _____ Location: _____

Pearl of Great Price

One of life's most costly and beautiful objects is born out of pain and irritation—the pearl. A tiny piece of sand slips into an oyster's shell and begins to rub against the soft tissue, causing irritation. In response to the irritation, the oyster produces a hard substance. This substance eventually develops into one of the world's most beautiful jewels—a lovely luminous pearl. In fact, the greater the irritation, the more valuable the pearl!

...

Many single women view themselves as ugly oyster shells lying on the beaches of life, beset with the trials and problems that come with not being married. To make matters worse, they compare their crusty exterior to all the beautiful seashells around them and wonder how any man could ever give his attention to them.

If you are one of these women, be encouraged. Don't view the trials of singleness as irritating grains of sand to be discarded as quickly as possible. Realize that God has them there to create something beautiful in you....

God is using the sands of singleness to make you perfect and complete. He's developing pearls of character in your life.

_____

_____

_____

_____

_____

_____

_____

_____

_____

_____

_____

_____

_____

_____

_____

_____

_____

_____

_____

_____

_____

_____

_____

The greater the irritation, the more valuable the pearl!

Day: _____ Date: _____ Time: _____ Location: _____

Virtue Is Irresistible

...If you attract a guy with only your looks, then you are headed for trouble, since looks don't last. As time goes on, we all end up looking like oysters. Therefore, what you look like on the inside is far more important than what you look like on the outside.

...What enabled Ruth to catch Boaz's attention? Was it her gorgeous hair or beautiful eyes? No! The answer is found in Boaz's response to her question in Ruth chapter 2.

> *Then she fell on her face, bowing to the ground and said to him,*
> *'Why have I found favor in your sight that you should take notice of*
> *me, since I am a foreigner?' And Boaz answered and said to her,*
> *'All that you have done for your mother-in-law after the death of*
> *your husband has been fully reported to me, and how you left your*
> *father and mother and the land of your birth, and came to a people*
> *that you did not previously know.* (Ruth 2:10-11).

Boaz was attracted to the virtue or character displayed in Ruth's life. A woman of virtue is irresistible to a godly man.

_____

_____

_____

_____

_____

_____

_____

_____

_____

_____

_____

_____

_____

_____

_____

_____

_____

_____

_____

_____

_____

_____

_____

_____

_____

_____

A woman of virtue is irresistible to a godly man.

Day: _____ Date: _____ Time: _____ Location: _____

Hannah More

Religion of the Heart

God is the fountain from which all streams of goodness flow. He is the center from which all rays of blessedness shine. All our actions are, therefore, only good insofar as they have a reference to Him: the streams must revert to their Fountain, the rays must converge again to their Center.

If love for God is the governing principle, this powerful spring will actuate all the movements of the reasonable creature. The essence of religious faith does not so much consist in actions as in affections. Though right actions may be performed where there are not right affections, they are a mere carcass, utterly devoid of soul, and therefore, of virtue. On the other hand, genuine affections cannot substantially and truly exist without producing right actions. Let it never be forgotten that a devout inclination which does not have life and vigor enough to ripen into action when the occasion presents itself has no place in the account of real goodness.

What a model for our humble imitation is that divine Person who was clothed with our humanity!

He dwelt among us so that the pattern might be rendered more engaging and conformity to it made more practicable. His life was one of unbroken, universal charity. He never forgot that we are compounded both of soul and body, and after teaching the multitude, He fed them. He repulsed none for being ignorant, was impatient with none for being dull, despised none for being loathed by the world, and He rejected none for being sinners. Our Lord encouraged those whose forgiveness others criticized; in healing sicknesses He converted souls; He gave bread and forgave injuries. Christians must seek to express their morning devotions in their actions through the day.

(Hannah More, *The Religion of the Heart*, [Burlington, New Jersey: D. Allinson & Co., 1811], updated by Donald L. Milam, Jr., pp. 27, 33, 85-86, as cited in Tommy Tenney, *Mary's Prayers and Martha's Recipes* [Shippensburg, Pennsylvania: Fresh Bread, 2002], pp. 18-19)

_____

_____

_____

_____

_____

_____

_____

God is the fountain from which all streams of goodness flow.
He is the center from which all rays of blessedness shine.

Day: _____ Date: _____ Time: _____ Location: _____

Inward Beauty

The key to beauty is found in First Peter 3:4 (NIV): "Instead, it should be that of your inner self, the unfading beauty of a gentle and quiet spirit, which is of great worth in God's sight." This kind of beauty can only get better the older it gets....

When you look at the virtuous woman of Proverbs 31:10-31, you will see God's picture of a beautiful woman. There are 20 verses describing her. Only one verse mentions her outward appearance. If you were to spend 1/20 of your time on outward physical beauty and the other 19/20 on developing the other qualities God describes as beautiful, such as wisdom, kindness, and godliness, you would become the excellent woman Proverbs 31:10 says a man should try to find.

...King Solomon said in Proverbs 31:30 (NIV)..."Charm is deceptive, and beauty is fleeting; but a woman who fears the Lord is to be praised." There are many women who fear pimples, wrinkles, flabby thighs, and crow's feet, but very few women who really fear the Lord. With which are you attractive to men: the snares of Proverbs 5, 6, and 7, or the beauty of First Peter 3:4?

_____

_____

_____

_____

_____

_____

When you look at the virtuous woman of Proverbs 31:10-31,
you will see God's picture of a beautiful woman.

Day: _____ Date: _____ Time: _____ Location: _____

Two-Way Conversation

Have you ever tried to develop an intimate relationship with Jana Jabberbox? She's the gal who has lots to say and loves to hear herself say it. You try to say something when she takes a breath—which isn't often—but she keeps right on talking. She never listens. It's a one-way conversation, and you are left out. Even when someone is very special to you, you do not get too excited with a steady monologue. Listening is an important part of developing a closeness with someone else. If you want to get to know the Lord, you must seek Him not only with a whole, clean, and pure heart, but also with a listening heart.

As you spend time with God during your daily devotional time, learn to listen to Him as you read of His love and thoughts about you in the Bible. Think about what He is saying to you personally. Sit silently and write what impressions come to your listening heart. As you read and study His love letters, the Bible, you begin to see what He really thinks of you and what wonderful plans He has for you. As a result, your devotion grows and grows.

_____

_____

_____

_____

_____

_____

_____

_____

_____

_____

_____

_____

_____

_____

_____

_____

_____

_____

_____

_____

_____

_____

_____

_____

If you want to get to know the Lord, you must seek Him not only with a whole, clean, and pure heart, but also with a listening heart.

Day: _____ Date: _____ Time: _____ Location: _____

Hannah Smith

The Lord Our Dwelling Place

'Lord, thou hast been our dwelling place in all generations.'

The comfort or discomfort of our outward lives depends more largely upon the dwelling place of our bodies than upon almost any other material thing; and the comfort or discomfort of our inward life depends similarly upon the dwelling place of our souls.

Our dwelling place is the place where we live, and not the place we merely visit. It is our home. All the interests of our earthly lives are bound up in our home; and we do all we can to make them attractive and comfortable. But our souls need a comfortable dwelling place even more than our bodies; inward comfort, as we all know, is of far greater importance than outward; and, where the soul is full of peace and joy outward surroundings are of comparatively little account.

It is of vital importance, then, that we should find out definitely where our souls are living. The Lord declares that He has been our dwelling place in all generations, but the question is, Are we living in our dwelling place? The psalmist says of the children of Israel that 'they wandered in the wilderness, in a solitary way; they found no city to dwell in. Hungry and thirsty, their soul fainted in them.' And I am afraid there are many wandering souls in the church of Christ, whom this description of the wandering Israelites would exactly fit. All their Christian lives they have been wandering in a spiritual wilderness, and have found no city to dwell in, and, hungry and thirsty their souls have fainted in them. And yet all the while the dwelling place of God has been standing wide open, inviting them to come in and take up their abode there forever. Our Lord Himself urges this invitation upon us. 'Abide in me,' He says, 'and I in you'; and He goes on to tell us what are the blessed results of this abiding and what are the sad consequences of not abiding.

The truth is, our souls are made for God. He is our natural home, and we can never be at rest anywhere else. "My soul longeth, yea, even fainteth for the courts of the Lord; my heart and my flesh crieth out for the living God.' We always shall hunger and faint for the courts of the Lord, as long as we fail to take up our abode there.

(Hannah Smith, *The God of All Comfort*, Ch. 8. 3 Jan. 2002
<http://www.ccel.org/s/smith_hev/comfort/htm/VIII.htm#VIII>)

The truth is, our souls are made for God. He is our natural home, and we can never be at rest anywhere else.

Day: _____ Date: _____ Time: _____ Location: _____

The Answer to Life

Whenever a single woman decides to abandon herself completely to Jesus, as Ruth did, she will find herself out of step with society and, sometimes even with her friends. A single woman today needs the boldness to challenge and break the cycle of the "American way" that exalts a relationship with a man as the answer to life. This "American way" blurs the reality of the ultimate answer to life found in a deep relationship with Jesus Christ...

Often a woman will attempt to find delight in a career if Mr. Right has not arrived. In time, even her "great career" will prove to be less than satisfying. A career, marriage, or even motherhood is not enough to totally satisfy you by itself. God knows that you will never be complete until you really understand that you are complete in Jesus. Colossians 2: 9-10 says, "For in Him all the fullness of Deity dwells in bodily form, ...and in Him you have been made complete, and He is the head over all rule and authority."

When a single woman enters a career or even marriage without understanding that she is complete in Christ, she will be disillusioned and dissatisfied.

_____

_____

_____

_____

_____

_____

_____
_____
_____
_____
_____
_____
_____
_____
_____
_____
_____
_____
_____
_____
_____
_____
_____
_____
_____
_____

*…the "American way" …exalts a relationship with a man
as the answer to life.*

Day: _____ Date: _____ Time: _____ Location: _____

Do You Believe the Lie?

Why do women feel they have to go after the men? Many women have believed a lie. They think, "I must get the best for myself because God may not give it to me." What do you think would have been the outcome of Ruth's life if she had chosen to believe this lie? Would she have returned home with Orpah and married one of the local guys? Would she have followed Naomi to a new land, but taken control of her own destiny in choosing a mate to care for herself and her mother-in-law?…

Ladies, God gives you the choice between His plans and yours. In the midst of her circumstances, Ruth could not have possibly seen that a man like Boaz would one day be her prince. Neither can you with your limited perspective see who or where your prince will be. Only God has all things in view.…Don't look back one day and regret that you made your "life mate" choice from a limited perspective because you longed for the security of a relationship. God can and will give you His best if you wait for it.

_____

_____

_____

_____

_____

_____

_____

_____

_____

_____

_____

_____

_____

_____

_____

_____

_____

_____

_____

_____

_____

_____

_____

_____

_____

_____

Only God has all things in view.

Day: _____ Date: _____ Time: _____ Location: _____

The Motive Check

...Before you go to another activity to spend time with the available guys, as you check your hair and makeup and teeth, give yourself a thorough "heart flossing."...A woman with selfish motivation mentally plots the next maneuver to capture the attention of the man of her dreams. Ask the Lord to reveal any impure motive that resides in your heart...This is not to say that you cannot do nice things for a man; it is simply a warning to check your motives...Before you bake one more thing for a brother or purchase one more book or meaningful card, be very careful to check your motive and honestly respond to whatever the Lord shows you. You can save yourself many tears and much frustration if you are just willing to do a regular "motive check" on your heart.

Manipulation and maneuvering can be deadly. If you maneuver to get a man, you will have to maneuver to keep him! This is not implying that there is no work involved in a good relationship, but there is a huge difference between working and maneuvering. You recognize the difference between the two by discerning your motive.

_____

_____

_____

_____

_____

_____

_____

_____

_____

_____

_____

_____

_____

_____

_____

_____

_____

_____

_____

_____

_____

_____

_____

_____

_____

_____

_____

*You can save yourself many tears and much frustration if you
are just willing to do a regular "motive check" on your heart.*

Additional copies of this book and other
book titles from DESTINY IMAGE are
available at your local bookstore.

For a complete list of our titles,
visit us at www.destinyimage.com
Send a request for a catalog to:

Destiny Image® Publishers, Inc.
P.O. Box 310
Shippensburg, PA 17257-0310

*"Speaking to the Purposes of God for This
Generation and for the Generations to Come"*